Seven Steps to Improve Your Child's Social Skills
A Family Guide

Kristy S. Hagar, PhD
Sam Goldstein, PhD
Robert Brooks, PhD

Illustrated by
Richard A. DiMatteo

Specialty Press, Inc.
Plantation, Florida

Library of Congress Cataloging-in-Publication Data

Hagar, Kristy S., 1966-
    Seven steps to improve your child's social skills: a family guide / Kristy S. Hagar, Sam Goldstein, Robert Brooks; illustrated by Richard A. DiMatteo.
      p. cm.
    Includes index.
    ISBN 1-886941-60-2 (alk. paper)
    1. Social skills in children. 2. Socialization. 3. Social skills—Study and teaching. 4. Parent and child. I. Goldstein, Sam, 1952- II. Brooks, Robert B. III. Title.

HQ783.H23 2006
302.3'4083--dc22

                                          2006044258

Cover design by Kall Graphics
Illustrations by Richard A. DiMatteo

10 9 8 7 6 5 4 3 2 1

Printed in the United States of America

Specialty Press, Inc.
300 Northwest 70th Ave., Suite 102
Plantation, Florida 33317
(954) 792-8100 • (800) 233-9273
www.addwarehouse.com

Dedication

For Janet, Allyson, and Ryan; and my friend John Snarr
S.G.

For Chuck and Rachel and Laura
K.H.

With love to Marilyn, Rich and Cybèle, Doug and Suzanne,
and Maya, Teddy, and Sophia
R.B.

Thanks to Kathleen Gardner for her editorial support
and to Harvey C. Parker for appreciating our ideas.
S.G.
K.H.
R.B.

Other Books in the Seven Step Family Guide Series

Seven Steps to Homework Success
Sydney Zentall and Sam Goldstein

Seven Steps to Help Your Child Worry Less
Sam Goldstein, Kristy Hagar, and Robert Brooks

Angry Children, Worried Parents:
Seven Steps to Help Families Manage Anger
Sam Goldstein, Robert Brooks, and Sharon Weiss

TABLE OF CONTENTS

Introduction

Let's take a walk down memory lane and think about our childhood social experiences. Think about the relationships you had with your family, your friends, your teachers, and your coaches. Think about the kids you knew. Some seemed to be natural leaders who always knew how to work a crowd; some were content with a few close friends and maintained those friendships for years; and some seemed to exist on the periphery, either not that interested in getting to know others or not knowing how to become more involved. You know from your childhood experience that children vary greatly in their social skills — and that childhood can be quite difficult for those who lack such skills.

You are probably reading this book because you have observed that your child struggles with friendships. You might have noticed that for your child, participating and engaging in everyday social interactions seems awkward, unsuccessful, or anxiety-provoking. And you're likely not sure why your child struggles with social interaction, or how you can help.

How important are social skills? Do you have to be a social butterfly to be successful in life? How do you know if you have the right amount of social skills? These questions might not have absolute answers, but we do know a lot about how an individual child's social skills can influence his ability to make and meet goals, build and maintain self-esteem, and develop a rewarding and fulfilling life surrounded by others.

A Walk Down Maple Street

Let's visit Maple Street. It could be a street in just about any city, a street populated by families with differing cultures, incomes, traditions, and social styles. Some are at ease in just about any social setting; others struggle, for various reasons, to develop and maintain social connections. We'll visit a few Maple Street households and describe some of the children living there.

101 Maple Street

John, a ten-year-old in fifth grade, sometimes has trouble talking to other kids. He has been diagnosed with Asperger's syndrome and is quite smart, but he is interested in only a few things. He has several friends in the neighborhood he's known since he was quite young, but when they come over to play he sometimes ignores them or can't understand why they don't want to talk about or play with his submarines.

147 Maple Street

Shannon is a twelve-year-old girl who is considered by most other kids in the neighborhood to be the bully on the block. She is abrasive and gets into fights frequently. She has a few friends but always seems to be directing them rather than interacting with them. Her mother complains that Shannon has "almost gone through the whole neighborhood" of friends because she can be hurtful, rude, and bossy.

123 Maple Street

In this house lives Jimmy, a shy and reserved seven-year-old. If you asked his parents, they'd say Jimmy has one friend he plays with regularly. He seems hesitant to try new things and feels anxious when anticipating being around other children or adults. As a young child, he used to hide behind his dad's legs at social events and reunions.

Seven Steps to Improve Your Child's Social Skills

Although the children living on Maple Street are very different in their personalities and social styles, they have one thing in common: difficulty interacting with their peers and lack of a comfortable connectedness to others. Your child most likely shares similar struggles.

This *Seven Steps* volume will help you understand and define basic social skills—such as those needed to make and keep friends, behave appropriately in small- or large-group settings, feel at ease when around others, and with minimal worry navigate social situations to achieve desired goals—and identify the reasons your child may be having trouble navigating the social system. It will also present some strategies that you can use to help your children develop better social skills. The seven-step process outlined in this book is not intended

127 Maple Street

A nine-year-old girl named Melanie lives here. She wants to have more friends but is socially awkward and clumsy. In her efforts to make friends, she sometimes is too pushy or has trouble picking up on hints from her peers.

to change your child's temperament or personality, but to help you guide her in developing skills to make social interactions more rewarding, less arduous, and less anxiety-provoking.

Step 1: Understand the Social Mindset and Its Significance

In Step 1 we define the different behaviors and skills that make up what we broadly refer to as a social mindset. We also discuss how thoughts, feelings, actions, and reactions influence social skills.

Step 2: Target Social Skills for Improvement

In this Step we help you identify when and how your child's social difficulties may be negatively affecting his self-esteem, his hopes and dreams, and his long-term adjustment. We discuss the emergence of social skills from a developmental perspective and explain what is and is not appropriate at various levels of development. We also provide an overview of several factors to consider that may be related to your child's difficulties, such as language development, motor skills, intellectual processing problems, learning disabilities, problems with self-discipline, or worried or helpless behavior. Finally, we present information on obtaining professional help, if it is needed.

Step 3: Help Your Child Become an Active Participant in the Process

In a perfect world, children would be willing to wholeheartedly accept their parents' loving advice and guidance. Unfortunately, many children aren't eager to get on board with Mom or Dad's advice, especially when it comes to something as potentially complex as redefining or changing how they interact with their peers. Step

3 will equip you to nurture an optimistic mindset in your child, as well as to destigmatize and demystify social skills problems. The Step also outlines how to create a plan with your child and gives tips for discussing thoughts, feelings, actions, and reactions.

Step 4: Employ Strategies to Improve Social Skills

In this Step, we address in greater detail how thoughts, feelings, actions, and reactions influence the success of social interactions. We offer a review of strategies for improving back-to-basics social skills: both nonverbal skills, such as eye contact, body language, and personal space, and verbal skills, such as listening, reciprocity, timing, and vocal quality.

Step 5: Practice Social Interactions

After learning the skills and strategies discussed in Step 4, the challenge is to use these tools in everyday life. In Step 5 we discuss making gradual gains, starting by providing feedback, structure, and practice within the family setting and then expanding to other social situations. The goal is to arm children with the techniques to assess social situations and make appropriate choices with the new skills they have learned and practiced.

Step 6: Assess and Solve Problems

Improving social skills often takes time and usually includes some discomfort, regression, or falls along the way. This Step highlights common roadblocks to improving social interactions, including dealing with parental frustrations or expectations for change. We will revisit some of the specific issues described in Step 2 that may be influencing your child's social skills and provide suggestions on how to address these potential problems.

Step 7: Nurture a Resilient Mindset in Your Child

This last step is perhaps the most important, as a resilient mindset is a crucial tool that can help children overcome difficulties or stressors they may encounter not only in childhood but in later years. Children who are confident and hopeful about their place in the world and about the support of those around them are better able to navigate the peaks and valleys of everyday life. Nurturing a child's islands of competence and providing a role model for responsibility, compassion, and social conscience are important parental goals. Letting your children know that mistakes and minor setbacks can occur while helping them understand that we can always learn from our mistakes helps instill hope and confidence for setting and mastering future goals.

Conclusion and Appendixes

This workbook closes with a conclusion and two appendixes, one for educators and one for health professionals who work with children with social skill problems. The appendixes provide suggestions and strategies to use this text to assist children with social needs. Resources are also provided to assist professionals with additional information on social skills programs or informative references.

Step 1

Understand the Social Mindset and Its Significance

Humans are social beings. For our first few years of life we are completely dependent on others to care for and nurture us. When we are alone, most of us long for the company of others. As the saying goes, no man is an island, and none of us can do without a social mindset. Very broadly defined, a *social mindset* consists of a unique set of thoughts, feelings, actions, and reactions we routinely use in our daily interactions with other human beings. This mindset is what guides children's decisions as they speak on the telephone, beg Mom and Dad to have a sleepover, excitedly await going to school to see friends, wait in line on the playground, and behave politely when receiving a not-so-great present from a family member. Although our social mindsets are largely shaped during childhood, they continue to change throughout our lives.

Our social mindset is composed of our *thoughts, feelings, actions,* and *reactions. Thoughts* reflect our internal dialogue, a running commentary within our heads about the interactions we have with others. These thoughts can foster positive or negative *feelings*. For example, if you think about how nice it was that you were invited to a party, you will probably experience a good feeling. Negative thoughts, such as anxiety and anger (which have been the focus of some of our other *Seven Steps* books), often foster negative feelings. When we think that we are dumb, bad, or incapable, we often feel bad.

Negative thoughts and feelings often lead to erroneous assumptions about others' motives and personalities. That is, if we interpret the innocent behavior of another individual as purposeful, we assume negative motives for their behavior, which leads us to assume negative attributes about them; for example, *He must have stepped on my foot on purpose—therefore he is not a very nice person.* Or, *He must have chosen to not call me rather than forgotten, so he doesn't care very much about other people.* Challenging negative thoughts, feelings, and assumptions is one of the many tools we will explore in developing a social mindset.

It is just a small step from thoughts and feelings to *actions*. Clearly, positive thoughts foster good feelings and set the stage for positive actions, while negative thoughts do the opposite. Actions can be verbal or nonverbal, positive or negative. (Later we will discuss body language, as well as verbal and nonverbal  communication.) Positive actions might include clapping when someone catches a ball and saying such encouraging words as, "Wow, you did a great job catching that ball!"

Reactions are our responses to others' attempts at social interaction. Reactions—just like thoughts, feelings, and actions—can be positive or negative. Examples of negative reactions include aggression, arguing, teasing, complaining, or bossing, whereas positive reactions could include cooperating, being assertive, offering a compliment, or helping others. Reactions are critical in maintaining social interaction. Let's go back to the example of complimenting someone on a good catch. What if the other child ignores the compliment? A positive reaction when ignored might be to speak a bit louder; a negative reaction might be to become angry and refuse to speak to the child. The reaction sets the tone for continuing social interaction and may help strengthen or weaken the social relationship.

An effective social mindset is required to navigate even the most benign social situations. We interact with others from the moment of birth, and in many respects our well-being depends on our ability to connect with, accept, and engage other human beings. A social mindset is critical to the existence of many nonhuman species as well. In a remarkable classic study by American psychologist Harry Harlow, young rhesus monkeys were separated from their mothers shortly after birth. They were provided substitute mothers made of either wire mesh or cloth. Harlow's monkeys preferred the artificial mother covered with cloth to the wire mother. They would drink a bottle from either mother, but when distressed the monkeys fed by a wire mother sat alone while those fed by the cloth mother sought comfort from the substitute. Harlow revealed that baby monkeys, too, require comfort and affection. Social interactions not only assist our survival but form the basis for our identity, self-esteem, satisfaction with life, and emotional well-being. When cut off from others, "solitary confinement" may be the greatest form of punishment human beings can endure.

It's easy to understand how social skills play a crucial part in your child's school, family, and community activities, or even in your own life. There have probably been times when you have wanted to tell a co-worker to go jump in a lake or tell a nosy aunt to mind her own business, but your social mindset enabled you to think through the potential negative outcomes of these activities and then choose among more effective strategies to accomplish a reasonable goal.

Social skills do not automatically turn on when children enter kindergarten, graduate from high school, or get their first job. Developing a social mindset is both nature and nurture: genetics lays a foundation, but life experience and our thoughts about our lives play a significant role. Some children do come into the world genetically and biologically better equipped to develop an effective social mindset, while other children are at a disadvantage socially. Children with autism, for example, struggle to understand and develop the rules of social interaction. But biology is not destiny, and with guidance and support every child can develop an effective social mindset. As parents, teachers, and professionals, we can adjust expectations and goals so as to help children develop a set of skills that may not be as easily learned for some as for others. Our mindset must be similar to teaching a poorly coordinated child to ride a bicycle: Practice will help develop proficiency. It's important to be patient and not set the bar too high initially, and to create an atmosphere in which the child feels comfortable making mistakes, learning from those mistakes, and developing more effective thoughts, actions, and reactions.

The path through childhood, adolescence, and adulthood can be difficult for some but can be more skillfully and comfortably negotiated with an effective social mindset and the support of family and friends. In Step 2 we will help you identify whether your child needs help building social skills. As you read the next few Steps, keep in mind the specific components of the social mindset (thoughts, feelings, actions, and reactions) to help you focus on when and if your child needs help, how to involve your child in the process of change, and how to target specific skills to develop.

Step 2

Target Social Skills for Improvement

Bob Dylan wrote, "You don't need a weatherman to know which way the wind blows." When children struggle socially their problems are easy for parents to observe but often very difficult to change. As counselors, when we ask parents of a child struggling socially how they know he has problems, we often hear such answers as, "No one plays with him," "He starts fights with others," and "He doesn't have any friends." Yet a more precise understanding of the reasons your child may struggle is required in order to help influence his social success and social mindset.

In this Step we will help you identify social problems that may be negatively influencing your child's self-esteem, hopes and dreams, and long-term adjustment. We begin by discussing social skills from a developmental perspective (that is, by age). This will give you a better understanding of whether your child's behavior, social development, and social interests are normally developed or unusual compared to peers. Once you

have defined specific areas of weakness, you can begin the journey of effectively shaping your child's social mindset.

The Uniqueness of Each Child

Our dreams and wishes for our children begin long before birth. We want them to have "ten fingers and ten toes," to be healthy. We want them to be happy, successful, and satisfied, and we certainly want them to form solid friendships and connections to others. But to love our children unconditionally is to accept them for who they are, not necessarily what we want them to be; and this acceptance includes their temperament and level of development. Parents discover quickly that each child possesses a unique in-born temperament. Some children are born with an easy temperament, and others are not.

A number of years ago, I (Sam Goldstein) was having lunch at a local restaurant when a young couple entered with an eight-month-old baby, their first child. The child was pleasant and outgoing, with a smile for everyone who passed. Within a few moments, people all around were patting him on the head and making eye contact. His parents boasted that they were going to have five children because "parenting is so easy." This child's temperamental style formed a foundation even at a young age to begin making positive connections with others.

About halfway through the meal a couple came in with a baby about the same age who was whining and inconsolable. Very quickly those sitting around this couple wished they would take their lunch elsewhere. Perhaps this child was having a bad day, or perhaps, temperamentally speaking, many days were bad days. These parents loved and cared for their child just as much as the first couple. Yet the difference in the children's temperament, even at this young age, was obviously making a difference in the way the children began forming connections with others and developing their social mindsets.

Even children reared within the same family can be completely different in their personalities, temperaments, dispositions, and achievements of various developmental milestones. Accepting your child's unique temperament and pattern of development doesn't mean you can't set goals and make changes in these qualities. Rather, acceptance allows you to set realistic goals and have appropriate expectations for change. In these cases, working with a professional (such as an educator, psychologist, or speech pathologist) is an important component of your plan to help your child develop an effective set of social skills and social mindset.

Developmental Milestones

Developmental milestones help us determine what is normal or expected behavior for a particular age. Although every child is unique, there are certain recognizable rules of child development, such as the following:

- *Development is predictable.* For example, children learn to sit up before they learn to crawl, and they learn to crawl before they learn to walk. They also take their first steps and say their first meaningful words at about the same time.

- *Developmental milestones are attained at about the same time in most children.* For example, most children begin walking and talking around the time of the first birthday.

- *Developmental opportunity is needed.* Children must be given the opportunity to use their skills in order to develop them appropriately.

- *Children progress through developmental phases.* Growth is not always consistent or even. It is well recognized that all children go through physical growth spurts, or periods when they seem to be growing and learning more rapidly than at other times.

- *Individuals differ greatly in development.* For example, individuality in language development depends on many factors, including heredity, nutrition, environment, and brain development.

Social and emotional milestones emerge very early in a child's development. By three months after birth, a baby can focus on faces, smile in response to a parent or caregiver's smile, and laugh or squeal. By four to six months of age, babies should respond to a simple game of peek-a-boo, start being more observant of voices and sounds, babble vowel–consonant combinations (ba-ba-ba), and respond to various facial expressions. By nine months babies start to consistently repeat gestures or play interactive games with caregivers, such as waving bye-bye or playing patty cake. They start to understand the word no and may start testing cause-and-effect (for example, observing what his parent does when he throws a toy). It is around this time that many children also develop stranger anxiety—clinging to a parent when around others (even those who are familiar, such as grandparents), fear or anxiety in settings away from home, and adamant protest when parents encourage interactions with others. By one year of age, some children are still somewhat wary of or uncomfortable with strangers, and this is completely developmentally appropriate. They do, however, continue their interactions with their parents or familiar caregivers, gain a greater awareness of how their actions influence others, and continue to experiment with vocalizations and sounds.

By age two, toddlers understand many words and can follow simple commands. They start to use simple phrases (such as "more juice") and can identify various objects, such as body parts, types of toys, and household items. They can refer to people by name, although their speech may be slightly difficult to understand. Toddlers at this age start to exhibit a greater desire to be around other children. They may start wanting to do what their older siblings are doing, and might demonstrate a greater awareness of social games and play. Toddlers at this age also display a higher level of protest when they are not allowed to participate in what they have set out to do, but can usually be redirected to something else rather quickly.

By age three, children's motor skills should be developed to the point that they can easily engage in physical play. They should be able to run, climb, and ride a tricycle or training bicycle. They often are able to communicate in four- to five-word sentences and to follow two- and three-step commands (although not always consistently). The development of consistent friendships starts to emerge over the course of a child's third year as they are able to request playmates and engage in reciprocal social play.

By age four, the preschooler should be able to speak in five- to six-word phrases and follow more complex directions. Reciprocal social play continues to evolve, and children develop a greater ability to role play and coordinate their play with multiple participants. They start to request greater independence in self-care skills, such as dressing, brushing teeth, and feeding. Their motor skills should be developed to the point that they can generally accomplish these tasks with minimal parental help or oversight.

By the age of five, children are preparing to begin school. Although knowledge can vary greatly among five-year-olds, most should be able to identify basic colors, count objects with one-to-one correspondence (up to about 10), and recognize numbers and letters. Children this age continue to engage in make-believe and imaginative play but can also participate in and stay focused on more organized activities that require a greater understanding of complex rules and co-operation, such as board games, hobbies, and sports.

With these general milestones in mind, you can begin to determine whether your child has met these milestones at a rate similar to her peers or if perhaps things are sufficiently different to warrant attention. The following decision tree will help you define your concerns and identify the types of activities that will benefit your child as well as help you determine if professional assistance is needed.

Decision Tree

1. **Did your child meet early social developmental milestones (under one year) appropriately?** For example, did he develop early social reciprocity (enjoyed playing patty cake, focused on a parent's face, cooed and babbled, smiled in response to a smile, enjoyed being hugged and cuddled) and an awareness of familiar versus unfamiliar people (including age-appropriate mild separation anxiety between eight and twelve months of age and mild distress or protest when separated from caregiver)?

❑ Yes ❑ No

If Yes, go to question 2. If No, consider these additional questions and then go to question 2.

Is your answer No because you have missed opportunities to observe these behaviors? (For example, perhaps your child has not been separated from you for any period of time.)

❑ Yes ❑ No

Before the age of two, did your child show interest in what siblings or other children were doing? Did he mimic them or engage in parallel play?

❑ Yes ❑ No

2. **By age three, did your child start to develop consistent friendships or attachments with others and seem comfortable and generally appropriate among familiar adults (such as family friends or close relatives)?**

❑ Yes ❑ No

If Yes, go on to question 3. If No, consider these additional questions and then go on to question 3.

Did your child's language and motor skills appear to develop at a rate similar to that of siblings or other children you know?

❑ Yes ❑ No

As a preschooler, did your child appear interested in what her siblings or other family members were doing, or did she prefer to do things on her own?

❑ Yes ❑ No

3. **By age six (or roughly first grade), did your child seem excited about going to school?** Was she able to talk about other kids in her class? Did she request sleepovers or play dates and get invited to birthday parties? Has your child's teacher made positive comments about her social interactions or skills?

❑ Yes ❑ No

If Yes, go on to question 4. If No, consider these additional questions and then go on to question 4.

Did any hesitancy on your child's part appear to be due to fear or worry about a specific situation that didn't interfere with other aspects of her life? (For example, your child was fearful about separating to go to pre-

school but had no problems socializing in other circumstances.)

❑ Yes ❑ No

Did hesitancy in your child appear to be part of a larger pattern of social isolation?

❑ Yes ❑ No

4. **Has your child developed normally according to the milestones discussed earlier, and does he now possess generally appropriate skills in many areas?** If some social difficulties are present, do they seem to be relatively new or isolated to certain situations?

❑ Yes ❑ No

If you answered Yes to Question 4 and to two or three of Questions 1-3, then this book is a good place to begin helping your child develop an effective social mindset. If several of your answers were No, then it is likely that you require additional, professional help. Seeking additional information about your child may be helpful. Discuss your concerns with other adults who interact with your child frequently. If your child is in school, speak to her teacher. Teachers often have a bird's-eye view of children's social interaction on a daily basis. If your concerns are reflected in the observations of others, particularly teachers, and you have answered No to at least two of the four questions above, then consultation with your pediatrician may be a good place to begin seeking a referral for a developmental psychologist or specialist capable of providing further evaluation and assistance. To get you started on this problem-solving process we will review a number of common problems that often interfere with the development of an effective social mindset.

Speech and Language Problems

Language is the window to the mind. It allows each human being to understand others and to be understood, so it is not surprising that language is a critically important skill for the development of an effective social mindset. The importance of language in developing appropriate social interaction is underscored by research demonstrating a significant pattern of social problems for children experiencing language delays. Sometimes these children are isolated and withdrawn. Other times they develop adverse coping strategies, such as aggression, in the face of a problem because their words are ineffective.

Language encompasses a broad constellation of skills, including *articulation* (how words are pronounced), *receptive* (understanding) and *expressive* (speaking) *vocabulary, semantics* (conveying meaning with language), and *pragmatics* (the use of language for social interaction). When a young child struggles with articulation or expressive language, her problems are easily observed by parents. However, problems such as those related to semantics or pragmatics may not be observed or understood as easily. When children struggle with these problems, many parents focus on behavior as the source of the problem rather than a weakness in underlying skills and abilities. When children struggle socially, a language screening should always be considered.

Communication is so essential to our nature that the inability to communicate often results in an array of undesirable behaviors, including poor social skills. Parents often sense that there is something wrong with their child's communication but have trouble explaining the problem. In fact, few people understand the process by which communication skills develop or the difference between speech and language. This distinction becomes important when we begin to examine the development of effective communication skills and the manner in which a child's failure to develop communication skills may affect socialization.

Communication is a broad term that is best described as a means by which we interact with others. Thus, communication forms the basis of social interaction. If children are communicating, they are having an effect on someone and creating an impact on their environment in some way.

Speech is the production of recognizable sounds combined in certain ways to make words. Speech involves the production of sounds as well as tone of voice, rate, rhythm, intonation, and many other aspects of sound production. The production of speech sound is often called articulation.

Language refers to a set of rules (such as grammar) used to convey ideas to others. Language tells us how to combine words to express ourselves and how to interpret what is said (receptive language). A set of rules called *syntax* tells us how to combine the words. Another set of rules, *semantics*, tells us how to express meaning through vocabulary. These two aspects of language have often been referred to as *form* and *content*. Form is the structure that keeps the content together, in much the same way that a glass holds liquid. It is important to understand the connection between communicating effectively and developing appropriate social skills. The connection begins early in life.

Language disorders in children result when certain prerequisite skills are lacking or delayed in developing. Hearing loss, for example, can impair a child's ability to receive or process the sounds of speech. A child may have difficulty making the correct speech sounds because of impairment in the speech mechanism or speaking muscles. Surprisingly, some children with normal hearing, intact speech mechanisms, and no apparent medical problem fail to develop speech and language as expected. These children often experience parallel problems in developing social skills.

In the first year of life, growth in communication and socialization takes place at an amazing rate. From the beginning children communicate in a variety of ways. Young infants are able to recognize their mother's voice and can use their body, eyes, and head to indicate recognition. Within the first six weeks, children widen or blink their eyes as an indication of arousal or startle in response to a loud noise. At about six weeks, children begin to shift their eyes and attempt to turn their heads in response to sounds. Young infants gradually become adept at using their eyes to locate the source of sounds. The ability to communicate progresses at a rapid rate. At six months of age, children begin to coo. They produce long vowel sounds and lots of gurgling, particularly in pleasurable situations, such as during feeding. By six months of age, children enter a new phase characterized by babbling and combining vowels and consonants. In this phase, a variety of sounds are produced and the development of speech sounds begins. Children spend more time making noises and seem to enjoy hearing themselves at this age.

By twelve months the first meaningful words (which don't always sound exactly like adult words) are spoken. Children at this age use a sound consistently in the same situation or to refer to a particular person or thing; this is recognized as the beginning of expressive language. Often, they begin by trying to name familiar objects and to imitate normal melody patterns. During this time, children begin to react to comments by adults such as "no", "hot," and "bye-bye." Children also understand single gestures, such as pointing, and respond to an increasing number of commands. They begin to express their needs and emotions by using words such as "more" and "no" in a variety of contexts. By twelve months of age, children recognize their own name and follow simple motor instructions (especially if accompanied by a visual cue), and many begin stringing words together.

By fifteen months of age, children can point and have at least a four- to six-word expressive vocabulary. By twenty months they rapidly increase vocabulary and begin to answer speech with speech. At this stage, foundational skills for socialization begin to emerge. Children mix single words in two-word sentences and gradually begin using three- and four-word sentences over the course of the next year or two. New words are learned and used every day. During this period, children begin to respond appropriately to complex statements and have a vocabulary of approximately twenty words. The ability to understand spoken language increases at a faster rate than the ability to produce speech.

The first two years of life are critical for the development of language processing (understanding) and language production (expression). Children's brains are rapidly developing the foundation for later skills needed to understand words and concepts as well as for possessing the fundamentals of communication. Children with deficient language skills may fail to receive important social and linguistic information. Thus, they may not know what is expected of them and may demonstrate inappropriate behavior. They may also be unable to express their needs and desires adequately and therefore learn to get what they need in other, often inappropriate, ways.

By twenty-four months of age children typically possess a vocabulary of two to three hundred words. They are able to name common objects and can speak in short, often incomplete, sentences. Speech and language skills develop and expand rapidly during the preschool years. By three years of age children typically can produce all vowels, possess a vocabulary of nine hundred to a thousand words, and speak three- to four-word sentences routinely. By four years of age most children are fully intelligible. They may not produce all sounds entirely correctly, but they can be easily understood. They also are able to ask many questions and use increasingly complex sentence forms. They can retell stories and talk about recent past events. They understand most questions about their immediate environment and things that have been of value for them.

By five years of age, children possess a two-thousand–word vocabulary. They can discuss their feelings and understand many concepts, such as right and left and today and tomorrow. They can follow three-step commands and typically have acquired about 80 percent of the grammar they will use as an adult. Finally, by seven years of age, children master all speech sounds and can routinely converse with children and adults.

Language involves learning the rules and using them in a communicative way for socialization. Children understand adult rules of grammar before they can use the rules themselves; that is, they comprehend the essence of what they are being told before they are fully expressive. Some children develop the ability to use the rules of language but for various reasons fail to comprehend the subtleties. They appear to have adequate language, especially as preschoolers, but begin to fall behind in their ability to understand and use language for effective communication, leading to social problems. They may fail to develop extended vocabulary or to understand how and why words are arranged in certain ways. They may be confused about the meaning of abstract words or about words that can have several meanings. Children with these types of comprehension problems might fail to follow directions unless given explicit information and may struggle to convey what they know. They may pass through first and second grade with little difficulty or with minor social problems, but as they move into third or fourth grade, when the social and communicative demands increase, they begin to experience failure in some academic and social areas. In a classroom these children may work well in a quiet one-on-one situation but struggle in groups. They often have trouble sorting through auditory and visual stimuli to determine what is important and what is not, so they have difficulty discerning appropriate behavior in the midst of what seems to them to be chaos. They may fail to meet social demands in an interpersonal setting and be viewed as odd or different.

To the untrained observer and even to many

trained professionals, these comprehension deficits masquerade as behavior problems. In social situations an inadequate understanding of the meaning of the words results in passivity and appears as noncompliance. Poor understanding of how and why words are sequenced in a certain way may result in confusion. What may look like noncompliance may actually be confusion over what is being requested. In social situations it is easy to understand how children with these problems are often perceived as lacking social skills when in fact they lack the basic linguistic skills necessary for effective socialization.

Motor Skills Problems

Children with delays in developing gross motor skills (large-muscle skills such as crawling, walking, running, and jumping) or fine motor skills (small-muscle skills such as self-feeding and manipulating and using toys) may also struggle with certain aspects of social interaction. They may have difficulty keeping pace with peers on the playground and therefore withdraw from physical activities. They may gradually start to avoid physical play, especially as the motor skills of their peers continue to develop. As educator Richard Lavoie points out, "last one picked is first one picked on." Researchers in Sweden have demonstrated that children with coordination problems often struggle to develop social skills and self-esteem. In many cases, motor deficits deprive children interested in and capable of effective social interaction of opportunities to build and develop skills and friendships.

Social Learning Disability

The term *social learning disability* (also referred to as *social learning problems*) was coined by Dr. Ami Klin of Yale University to describe the core problems experienced by children with autism and pervasive developmental disorders, which include Asperger's syndrome, Rett syndrome, and childhood disintegrative disorder. Many children with social learning disability possess average intelligence but struggle to develop interest in others and effective social skills. Some children with social learning disability are delayed in developing early language, although those with Asperger's often develop normal vocabularies but struggle to use their language skills for effective social communication.

There is a growing body of research demonstrating that although there is a biological (genetic) basis for social learning disability, with careful practice, guidance, and support, children with social learning disability can develop social skills and rewarding social relationships. This book's strategies to build an effective social mindset can be helpful as supportive interventions and teaching tools for these children. If you suspect your child has social learning disability, complete the following questionnaire. If you respond Yes to more than half of the questions, speak with your pediatrician, who may refer you to a psychologist or psychiatrist with expertise in the area of autism and pervasive developmental disorders.

Intellectual Processing Problems

Intelligence is an often misunderstood concept. Some tests of intelligence simply measure what children know, so a child taking this kind of test who has not been exposed to a wide range of information may get a result indicating intellectual deficiency. Other tests of intelligence mea-

Social Learning Disability Questionnaire

Name of child _____ Date _____

Person completing this form _____

My child . . .

- ❑ Yes ❑ No   1. talks excessively about favorite topics that hold limited interest for others.
- ❑ Yes ❑ No   2. uses words or phrases repetitively.
- ❑ Yes ❑ No   3. doesn't understand jokes.
- ❑ Yes ❑ No   4. interprets conversations literally.
- ❑ Yes ❑ No   5. frequently asks irrelevant questions.
- ❑ Yes ❑ No   6. experiences difficulty with conversational skills.
- ❑ Yes ❑ No   7. avoids or limits eye contact.
- ❑ Yes ❑ No   8. exhibits limited facial expression.
- ❑ Yes ❑ No   9. doesn't appear to understand basic social behavior.
- ❑ Yes ❑ No   10. misses social cues.
- ❑ Yes ❑ No   11. exhibits a strong negative reaction to change in routine.
- ❑ Yes ❑ No   12. engages in obsessive behavior.
- ❑ Yes ❑ No   13. displays an extreme or obsessive interest in a narrow subject.
- ❑ Yes ❑ No   14. lacks organizational skills.
- ❑ Yes ❑ No   15. is passively inattentive.
- ❑ Yes ❑ No   16. overreacts to normal sensory information.
- ❑ Yes ❑ No   17. limits self to certain clothing or foods.
- ❑ Yes ❑ No   18. appears clumsy or uncoordinated.

Intellectual Processing Skills Questionnaire

Name of child _____ Date _____

Person completing this form _____

During the past two months, how often did my child . . .

	Always	Usually	Sometimes	Never
1. work in a well-organized and neat way?	_____	_____	_____	_____
2. use strategies and plans when doing work?	_____	_____	_____	_____
3. evaluate his own behavior?	_____	_____	_____	_____
4. think before acting?	_____	_____	_____	_____
5. have many ideas about how to do things?	_____	_____	_____	_____
6. show self-control?	_____	_____	_____	_____
7. perform well on spatial activities (such as maps and diagrams)?	_____	_____	_____	_____
8. understand how things go together?	_____	_____	_____	_____
9. see the big picture?	_____	_____	_____	_____
10. understand complex verbal instructions?	_____	_____	_____	_____
11. work well with patterns?	_____	_____	_____	_____
12. like to use visual materials?	_____	_____	_____	_____
13. focus well on one thing?	_____	_____	_____	_____
14. work without being distracted by people or noises?	_____	_____	_____	_____
15. pay close attention?	_____	_____	_____	_____
16. listen to instructions without being distracted?	_____	_____	_____	_____
17. work well for a long time?	_____	_____	_____	_____
18. work well in a noisy environment?	_____	_____	_____	_____
19. work well with information in sequence?	_____	_____	_____	_____
20. do well with things presented step by step?	_____	_____	_____	_____
21. remember the order of information?	_____	_____	_____	_____
22. understand directions presented in sequence?	_____	_____	_____	_____
23. do well working with sounds in order?	_____	_____	_____	_____
24. closely follow directions presented in order?	_____	_____	_____	_____

From *Helping Children Learn* by Jack Naglieri and Eric Pickering. Used with permission.

sure the underlying processes necessary for effective learning. Children who develop these processes at a slower rate than others gradually fall behind their peers and eventually have below average intelligence or, in extreme cases, mental retardation.

There are four basic intellectual processing skills. *Planning processes* reflect the ability to make decisions about how to best complete tasks, use good strategy, control behavior, self-monitor, and self-correct. *Simultaneous processes* require the ability to relate parts to a group or whole, understand relationships among pictures and words, and work with nonverbal information. *Attention processes* reflect the ability to pay attention and concentrate, to focus on specific features of information and resist reacting to distracting information. *Successive (sequencing) processes* allow one to work with information in a specific linear order.

Children with slower development typically demonstrate interests in social skills consistent with their level of intellectual development rather than their age. For example, a six-year-old with low intelligence may demonstrate social skills and interests consistent with those of a four- or five-year-old. When parents of such a child adjust their expectations and provide social experiences appropriate for the child's developmental level, these children often do well. However, it is often the case that "slow isn't fast enough," as psychologist Dr. Joan Goodman has observed. When children struggle to keep pace developmentally with their chronological age, unrealistic expectations placed on them by family, peers, and teachers can create behavioral and emotional problems.

If you suspect your child has problems with intellectual processes, complete the questionnaire on page 19. Read each question and put a checkmark under the word that indicates how often you observed the behavior. If you answer Sometimes or Never to more than half of the questions, consider speaking with your child's teachers and requesting an evaluation by the school psychologist.

Learning Disabilities

Children with learning disabilities are not simply slow learners or weak intellectually; rather, they struggle with a number of basic skills necessary for efficient learning. Learning disabilities fall in two broad categories: *Auditory-verbal* and *visual-motor*. Each category consists of basic rote (automatic) skills and higher-order conceptual abilities. Auditory-verbal skills allow the understanding of meaningful language, as well as the use of language to reason and solve problems. Rote auditory-verbal skills include the abilities to develop language labels and appropriate associations, to retrieve information quickly, and to sequence. Rote visual-motor skills involve nonverbal abilities such as hand-eye coordination, writing, and assembling puzzles. Conceptual visual-motor abilities include social insight and reasoning, understanding math concepts, and nonverbal problem solving. Children with weakness in this area are often described as having a nonverbal learning disability.

Children with a nonverbal learning disability typically display a significant weakness in nonverbal skills; they often struggle to pick up on subtle or complex social cues and to comprehend how their actions and behavior influence others. This makes it difficult to navigate their social environment effectively. If you suspect that your child may have a learning disability,

Learning Disabilities Questionnaire

Name of child _____ Date _____

Person completing this form _____

Auditory-Verbal Skills

My child . . .

❑ Yes ❑ No   1. has trouble rhyming words.
❑ Yes ❑ No   2. has difficulty pronouncing sounds.
❑ Yes ❑ No   3. has trouble learning letter–sound associations.
❑ Yes ❑ No   4. has difficulty learning the days of week and months of year in sequence.
❑ Yes ❑ No   5. has difficulty recalling information.
❑ Yes ❑ No   6. has trouble sounding out unfamiliar words when reading.
❑ Yes ❑ No   7. has trouble ordering sounds in the correct sequence when spelling.
❑ Yes ❑ No   8. reads at a slow rate.
❑ Yes ❑ No   9. develops language slowly.
❑ Yes ❑ No   10. struggles to understand directions.
❑ Yes ❑ No   11. struggles to sustain conversation.
❑ Yes ❑ No   12. struggles to organize thoughts and ideas.
❑ Yes ❑ No   13. often forgets what has been read.
❑ Yes ❑ No   14. has trouble remembering concepts.
❑ Yes ❑ No   15. has trouble answering questions.

Visual-Motor Skills

My child . . .

❑ Yes ❑ No   1. forgets how letters look.
❑ Yes ❑ No   2. confuses letters with similar appearance.
❑ Yes ❑ No   3. reverses letters when writing.
❑ Yes ❑ No   4. transposes letters when reading or writing (e.g., *on* or *no*).
❑ Yes ❑ No   5. has trouble remembering how words look.
❑ Yes ❑ No   6. spells the same word in different ways.
❑ Yes ❑ No   7. spells words as they sound.
❑ Yes ❑ No   8. dislikes playing with construction toys.
❑ Yes ❑ No   9. struggles to tell time.
❑ Yes ❑ No   10. reads slowly.
❑ Yes ❑ No   11. has trouble putting puzzles together.
❑ Yes ❑ No   12. has difficulty distinguishing between left and right.
❑ Yes ❑ No   13. has difficulty understanding math concepts.
❑ Yes ❑ No   14. has trouble making a mental picture of information.

Adapted from *Learning Disabilities and Challenging Behaviors* by Nancy Mather and Sam Goldstein. Used with permission.

complete the questionnaire on page 21. The first part focuses on auditory-verbal abilities, the second part on visual-motor skills. If you answer Yes to more than half of the questions, speak with your child's teacher and request an evaluation by the school psychologist.

Problems with Self-Discipline

Children struggling to develop self-discipline are often impulsive and don't consistently think before they act, failing to weigh the consequences of their actions and plan future actions. They may understand a rule but are unable to use the rule to govern their behavior. Not unexpectedly, this often causes significant problems in the social arena. Often this pattern of impulsivity is accompanied by attention and activity problems. Children with inefficient self-discipline are often described as inattentive. They don't attend well to repetitive, effortful, or uninteresting activities. They have difficulty screening out distractions and are often distracted by inner thoughts. It is hard for them to know what to pay attention to, so in social situations they may seem odd or atypical. They have difficulty beginning activities, sustaining attention until the activity is completed successfully, and focusing attention on two events simultaneously. They are capable of paying attention but do not do so consistently, predictably, or efficiently.

Children struggling to develop self-discipline also have difficulty inhibiting physical activity. That is, they have trouble sitting still and are often viewed as restless or overactive. They also struggle to delay rewards. They tend to require immediate, frequent, predictable, and meaningful rewards. Inconsistent rewards result in most tasks being left unfinished. They often appear to require many more successful trials before a new behavior can be self-directed.

Finally, children struggling with self-discipline tend to be excessively emotional. They express the extremes of their emotions faster and with greater intensity than is age appropriate. They become frustrated quickly over minor events. Everyone around them is well aware of their presence and current feelings.

This constellation of problems symptomatically is referred to as *attention deficit hyperactivity disorder (ADHD)*. It is not the intent of this volume to provide diagnostic information concerning this or any other disorder. If you suspect that your child might have ADHD, we suggest you speak with your pediatrician or seek assessment from a psychologist or psychiatrist. Keep in mind that children with self-discipline problems can often verbalize appropriate social behavior and problem-solving skills but because of their limitations struggle to do what they know is right in everyday situations. Review the following checklist to help identify possible symptoms related to problems with self-discipline.

Worried and Helpless Behavior

Worry is a normal response in many situations. Mild worry can be a motivator to take action, such as preparing for a social activity, and it may also serve the interests of self-preservation. But excessive worry can interfere with positive social behavior. A child who worries lacks confidence in her ability to predict outcomes, which adversely affects her relationships. Further, as children worry about a particular social event they often begin to feel increasingly helpless or hopeless about their ability to do anything effective to solve the problem.

The easiest way to resolve worry is to avoid the worrisome situation, and in the social realm,

Self-Discipline Questionnaire

Name of child _____ Date _____

Person completing this form _____

My child . . .

❑ Yes ❑ No   1. fails to pay attention to details; makes frequent mistakes on schoolwork and tasks.

❑ Yes ❑ No   2, struggles to pay attention to tasks that are effortful or boring.

❑ Yes ❑ No   3. has difficulty following directions or instructions consistently; gets side-tracked.

❑ Yes ❑ No   4. has trouble organizing tasks, chores, projects, or activities.

❑ Yes ❑ No   5. loses things necessary for tasks or activities.

❑ Yes ❑ No   6. has trouble focusing on things; gets easily distracted by sights, sounds, or own thoughts.

❑ Yes ❑ No   7. seems forgetful; needs frequent reminders for things that should be well learned.

❑ Yes ❑ No   8. has difficulty sitting still, especially when required to (e.g., school, church).

❑ Yes ❑ No   9. struggles to wait her turn; interrupts others frequently.

❑ Yes ❑ No   10. seems frequently "on the go" or needs to move constantly.

❑ Yes ❑ No   11. talks excessively.

❑ Yes ❑ No   12. often seeks out others for entertainment; has difficulty playing by self or engaging in solitary tasks or activities.

❑ Yes ❑ No   13. seems restless and fidgety; tends to jump from one activity to the next.

From: *Seven Steps to Improve Your Child's Social Skills* by K. Hagar, S. Goldstein, and R. Brooks. This page may be reproduced.

Worried and Helpless Behavior Questionnaire

Name of child _____ Date _____

Person completing this form _____

My child . . .

❑ Yes ❑ No   1,   persistently talks about or seems preoccupied with a particular stressor or feared object or situation.

❑ Yes ❑ No   2.   seems to have changed sleeping habits in response to worrisome thoughts or events.

❑ Yes ❑ No   3.   avoids activities or situations that were previously enjoyed (e.g. competing in sports, going to school, going out in public).

❑ Yes ❑ No   4.   often complains of headaches or stomachaches in anticipation of an event or situation.

❑ Yes ❑ No   5.   cries or seems bothered by "little things"; is irritable or fussy.

❑ Yes ❑ No   6.   seems jumpy or tense, "on pins and needles."

❑ Yes ❑ No   7.   avoids activities away from home, such as sleepovers with friends or visits to familiar places.

❑ Yes ❑ No   8.   is hesitant to go to school or seems less enthusiastic about school.

❑ Yes ❑ No   9.   spends less time with friends, chooses (or avoids) activities that result in isolation from peers.

❑ Yes ❑ No   10.   has a decreased appetite or complains of not being hungry.

❑ Yes ❑ No   11.   displays tantrums, anger, or panic when pressed or encouraged to participate in previously enjoyed activities.

that often means avoiding other children. One particular kind of worry related to social situations, often referred to as *social anxiety*, is particularly important for this book. Concern about performing, interacting, or being embarrassed in social situations is probably one of the most common and normal worries that humans experience at one time or another. Common childhood social concerns include many of the same situations adults worry about, such as speaking before a group. Performance anxiety becomes social anxiety when the fear or worry is persistent and leads to certain behaviors such as crying, avoidance, or isolation, which, because it relieves worry, tends to increase over time, creating a higher hurdle for the child to overcome in the future.

If you are concerned that your child might struggle with worry, review the worry questionnaire on page 24. If you identify several symptoms as being consistently demonstrated in your child's behavior, we recommend discussing these concerns further with your child's pediatrician or perhaps the school counselor.

Defining Your Child's Social Skills and Mindset

The following assessment has two parts. Part I asks you to respond Yes or No to basic patterns of behavior. This will provide an overview of primarily negative social behaviors. Part II asks you to rate a basic set of social skills for your child. Take your time in completing this questionnaire. Seek input from other adults who interact with your child on a regular basis. Your answers to this survey will help you target specific social skills to work on with your child.

Finally, note that you might want to make copies of the blank form in order to share with other adults you enlist to help your child improve social skills (this is discussed in greater detail in Step 5).

Tackling the Problem

With an understanding of typical development, social skills, and your child's development, you can begin the process of change. It's vital that your mindset include an understanding that your child is unique, and so is the rate at which he can change. Particularly in the social arena, slow but positive progress is fast enough. It is difficult to transform a reserved, shy child into a gregarious social butterfly. It is equally difficult to help an impulsive child rein in his overly boisterous interactions with peers or to help a child with social learning disability understand how others think and feel. Your goal should not be to change your child's temperament or disposition but to teach her to navigate the social world, feel comfortable, and derive pleasure from connecting to and interacting with others. Just as we would want to foster a child's innate interest in music or art by providing lessons to develop skills, children who want to connect with others but can't do so successfully can benefit from lessons and instruction. Even if a child has reached a point where he has seemingly given up on friendships, with patience and support changes can be made.

Fortunately, as we will discuss in the next Steps, the opportunities to learn, develop, and practice social skills are ever present. You can become a coach and a cheerleader to reinforce the positive gains your child can demonstrate

Social Skills Assessment

Name of child _____ Date _____

Person completing this form _____

Part I
Read the description of each item and check the answer that best describes your child's abilities.

❑ Yes ❑ No   1. appears socially isolated, spending a large proportion of time engaged in solitary activities.

❑ Yes ❑ No   2. interacts less with others, appearing shy, timid, or overanxious.

❑ Yes ❑ No   3. complains of having no one to play with.

❑ Yes ❑ No   4. spends less time involved with other children due to an apparent lack of social skills.

❑ Yes ❑ No   5. has fewer friends than others due to negative, bossy, or annoying behaviors.

❑ Yes ❑ No   6. has fewer friends than others due to awkward or bizarre behaviors.

❑ Yes ❑ No   7. disturbs others by teasing, provoking, fighting, or interruptions.

❑ Yes ❑ No   8. is argumentative and needs to have the last words in verbal exchanges.

❑ Yes ❑ No   9. is aggressive toward others.

❑ Yes ❑ No   10. manipulates or threatens.

Part II
For each item, indicate the level of skill your child exhibits, using the scale below.

1 Very poor at this skill   2 Average at this skill   3 Exhibits this skill better than others

_____ demonstrates empathy.

_____ demonstrates the capacity for humor.

_____ expresses frustration and anger effectively.

_____ gains access to ongoing activities with peers.

_____ asserts rights and needs appropriately.

_____ expresses wishes and preferences clearly.

_____ approaches others positively.

_____ shares.

_____ plays games successfully with others.

_____ works cooperatively with peers.

_____ offers help to others.

_____ begins a conversation appropriately.

_____ listens during conversation.

_____ ends a conversation appropriately.

_____ asks questions appropriately.

_____ says "please" and "thank you."

_____ apologizes when a mistake is made

_____ accepts a compliment.

_____ gives a compliment.

_____ interprets body language.

_____ seeks help from others appropriately.

_____ joins an ongoing activity with others.

_____ takes turns appropriately.

_____ compromises with others appropriately.

_____ maintains eye contact when interacting with others.

_____ recognizes appropriate personal space when approaching others.

From: *Seven Steps to Improve Your Child's Social Skills* by K. Hagar, S. Goldstein, and R. Brooks. This page may be reproduced.

Social Skills Target Worksheet

Name of child _____ Date _____

Person completing this form _____

Part I

Look at all of the items listed in Part I of the Social Skills Assessment that you answered Yes. Choose the three most problematic or concerning items and write them in the space provided. (In Step 3 we'll discuss how to approach this worksheet in partnership with your child.)

1. _____

2. _____

3. _____

These are concerns viewed as causing significant difficulty with your child's social success, and they will help provide a framework for choosing the skills in the second part of this worksheet.

Part II

Now review Part II of the Social Skills Assessment and list up to five skills in the space provided below that you consider to be your child's strengths (in other words, those you answered as 2 or 3). These will be used as the initial building blocks to help foster a more successful and effective social mindset.

1. _____

2. _____

3. _____

4. _____

5. _____

Finally, list up to three of the skills that you rated as 1 on the second part of the Social Skills Assessment and that seem to relate best to the three concerns listed in Part I of this worksheet. These will be the initial skills to target in Step 3.

1. _____

2. _____

3. _____

From: *Seven Steps to Improve Your Child's Social Skills* by K. Hagar, S. Goldstein, and R. Brooks. This page may be reproduced.

daily. For some children, positive gains may be to ultimately accomplish asking a friend for a sleepover and having the visit go well. For others, positive gains might be to consistently demonstrate eye contact when talking to others or to not interact so aggressively that other children don't want to play.

Although you may be concerned about your child's social skills, there are a million and one things you would never want to change in your child. It is these individual personality and character strengths that serve as guideposts to help you foster your child's comfort in social settings and ultimately develop an effective social mindset. With these strengths in mind, as well as with the Social Skills Assessment at hand, the Social Skills Target Worksheet below will help serve as a framework for an initial plan of action.

Summary

In this Step we defined basic social skills and the ages at which they are typically mastered. We also highlighted several developmental and psychological issues that often influence the development of social skills and provided a series of checklists to help you identify whether your child struggles with any of those issues. Finally, we encouraged you to consider that your mindset is to help your child improve his comfort in the social realm and not to replace or vastly change his temperament or disposition. You are now ready to begin the journey of helping your child develop an effective social mindset. Keep your completed Social Skills Target Worksheet at hand as you read the next few chapters. In the next Step we will offer strategies to help you involve your child in the process and provide suggestions to target specific social skills and develop goals for progress.

Step 3

Help Your Child Become an
Active Participant in the Process

A basic characteristic of emotional well-being and resilience is the ability to distinguish between what we can and cannot control and to focus our energies on those areas that are within our power to change. When children lack particular thinking, language, temperament, and emotional management abilities, their social behaviors are likely to trigger ongoing negative feedback from peers and adults. These youngsters are often bewildered and uncertain why others appear angry with them or do not include them in activities. Not only are many unaware of the impact their behaviors have on others, but even if they have some appreciation of this impact, they are limited in modifying these social behaviors given their cognitive, language, temperament, and emotional management abilities. For this reason, it is very important for you to understand and appreciate your child's abilities. Unanswered questions raised in Step 2 should be addressed with a professional.

The confusion that pervades their daily lives makes it difficult for them to develop a belief that they are in control of their own destiny. Instead, they often feel overwhelmed or scared. They may blame others for their plight or view themselves as defective. One eight-year-old girl with social skills problems said, "I try to be nice, but no one seems to like me. No one wants to eat with me at school. The other kids aren't nice." Then, with an air of desperation, she added, "And I don't know how to get them to be nice."

Nurturing an Optimistic Mindset: A Feeling of Control

If we want our children to deal successfully with social challenges, we must reinforce an optimistic mindset, one characterized by realistic hope and a belief that problems are surmountable. A guiding principle in helping children develop this mindset is to involve them as much as possible in the process of managing, rather than being enslaved by, their feelings and thoughts. The extent and nature of the involvement will vary from one child to the next depending on such factors as the child's developmental and cognitive level and language skills, but even a small degree of participation can be significantly helpful. Let's examine some of the things you can do as a parent to reinforce a feeling of optimism and control in your child.

Being Empathic

A crucial first step is to practice empathy. As much as possible, we must place ourselves in our children's shoes and see the world through their eyes. In the process of helping a child deal with social skills problems, empathic parents ask several important questions, including the following.

In anything I say or do with my child, what do I hope to accomplish? In a situation that involves nurturing social skills, one of the main goals would be to help children become more aware of their behaviors and to learn strategies for developing more effective ways of interacting with others.

Am I saying or doing things in a way in which my child is most likely to listen to and learn from me and feel I really care? In answering this question it is crucial to be aware of the ways your child processes information. For example, if your child has receptive language problems, you must frequently seek feedback from your child during verbal exchanges. Sometimes we think we're speaking clearly, and we may be, but at a level beyond the child's comprehension. If you do not communicate with your child's needs in mind, your words may be experienced by your child as if you were speaking in a foreign language. We must meet children at their level of abilities lest further anger and confusion ensue.

Would I want anyone to behave or speak to me the way I am behaving or speaking to my child? This question should prompt us to reflect on our interactions with our children. For example, in response to a child not responding to suggestions, many well-meaning but frustrated parents might utter such comments as "If you listened to me you would understand what I'm saying," or "You keep interrupting before I finish, and I bet that's what you do with kids and that's why they don't like being with you," or "You have to try to remember what I'm telling you so you don't do the same thing again." These statements fail to validate what the child is experiencing. Many children with social skills deficits would love to improve their communication and interpersonal skills, but they don't know how. To suggest that they modify their behavior without providing them concrete techniques that fit their abilities can evoke anger and make them less likely to listen to you. Think about the following for a moment: If you were having difficulty relating with certain individuals at work, would you find it helpful if a friend said, "You wouldn't have these problems if you changed what you are doing, but for some reason you don't seem to want to change"? Being empathic does not imply that you fail to set limits on behavior in your children, but rather you do so in a way so that they learn from you rather than resent you.

How would I want my children to describe me when I attempt to help them deal with social problems, and how would they actually describe me? If you want your child to cooperate with you, she must sense that you understand her distress and that you are her ally, not her critic. When she voices frustration or demonstrates anger, you must convey to her that you know kids get upset when other kids pick on them or they have no friends, but we have to figure out the best way for her to learn how to get along so she will begin to make friends. If appropriate, it can be helpful to share a time when you were a child and had difficulty with peers and how you learned to deal with the situation. If children experience us as empathic, they are more likely to join in the process of strengthening social skills.

Destigmatizing and Demystifying Social Skills Problems

It is difficult to struggle with loneliness, teasing, frustration, and anger. The burden is intensified when accompanied by beliefs that add to the child's sense of distress. For instance, even youngsters prone to blame others may be concerned that their problems have made their parents unhappy or that they have disappointed their parents; some are embarrassed and believe that there is something wrong with them, that they are unlovable, while others believe that they are all alone and no one else has experienced the pain and anger that they have.

As parents, we must become as knowledgeable as possible about the sources of our children's social skills difficulties and then use this information with our children in a nonjudgmental, supportive manner. Because every child is

different, an important step to demystify and destigmatize your child's behavior is to understand his perception of events and his feelings about his actions. With this understanding you can reassure your child that many youngsters have problems with peers and feel angry and lonely, but that there are ways to get along better. It is important for children to feel that their parents will help them with practical, realistic recommendations for relating to others. It is also important for children to feel that they are active participants in confronting their problems, which is not always easy when they lack certain abilities.

Creating a Plan with Your Child

Once you and your child have made the commitment to improve social skills, it is time to develop a plan. Steps 4 and 5 will describe ways to develop and implement a plan with well defined strategies for teaching social skills. Your particular plan will be based on the situation, your child's abilities, and the ways in which the social skills difficulties are expressed.

For instance, if we look at two children on Maple Street, Jimmy and Shannon, different interventions are indicated. Jimmy is the shy, reserved seven-year-old who appears to have been born with a shy, cautious temperament.

He becomes anxious around other people but does have one friend he plays with regularly. In Jimmy's case in might be helpful to use what we labeled *environmental engineering* in our book *Raising Resilient Children*, that is, designing situations that will help Jimmy to become less anxious and better equipped to handle interpersonal relationships.

Jimmy's parents might suggest that he invite his one friend over to play. (Most likely, they would make the actual phone call to the friend's parents.) They could help Jimmy plan for the visit by reviewing different activities or games he and his friend like to play. They can provide Jimmy with feedback after the friend's visit. As Jimmy learns to deal more successfully with this one peer, the parents might encourage him to invite another classmate or child in the neighborhood to their home so that he can begin to expand the number of friendships in his life.

In contrast to the hesitant Jimmy, twelve-year-old Shannon attempts to dominate relationships in an abrasive, bullying style. While Shannon's and Jimmy's behaviors are very different, they share interpersonal styles or social skills that work against the establishment of satisfying relationships. Children such as Shannon who rely on bullying often become defensive when anyone attempts to discuss their problems with them. They are prone to externalize responsibility for any difficulties. Consequently, in creating a plan with Shannon, her parents must be especially sensitive to how quickly she might dismiss their concerns, blame others, or deny problems. They have to present their concerns in an empathic, nonjudgmental way and recognize that their first attempt may be rejected by their daughter. For example, they might say, "Shannon, we've noticed something that we would like to talk about with you and help you with. It seems that a lot of the kids you play with don't seem to want to play with you after a while." If Shannon disagrees or says she doesn't care, her parents might respond, "We know it doesn't seem to be a problem, but it might be, and there may be ways of helping to make it better."

Her parents can share with Shannon some specific behaviors they have observed. They can say to her, "We know you feel that the other kids aren't being nice, but there may be things that you can do to have a better time with some of the kids who would like to be nice." This is a nonaccusatory statement that does not challenge Shannon's perceptions, but rather validates her beliefs about the reasons for her difficulties with her peers. Validation does not suggest you agree with your child, but simply that you understand the child's stated viewpoint. In addition, the parents are establishing the foundation for Shannon taking more responsibility for her behavior by enlisting her in considering ways of dealing with the problem.

It is also important when plans are designed to convey the message that if the plan is not successful, other approaches can be considered and implemented. Many children become discouraged when they attempt a strategy and it fails. This may elicit feelings of hopelessness, resulting in their giving up. Preparing them for the possibility that a plan may not work reassures children that mistakes or failures are experiences to learn from rather from than proof of loss or defeat.

The social difficulties encountered by Jimmy and Shannon are as different as their abilities are. These differences dictate different ways of approaching the problems they face, but for both children the use of empathy, identifying the issues involved, and inviting their participation in creating a plan of action are important aspects of any intervention.

The Social Autopsy

The benefits of involving children in creating a plan that will improve their social cognition and their relationships with others is illustrated by the *social autopsy*, a powerful strategy developed by our close colleague Richard Lavoie and described in detail in his recently published book *It's So Much Work to Be Your Friend: Helping the Learning Disabled Child Find Social Success*.

The social autopsy is based on the following key beliefs:

- Most social skill mistakes are not intentional.
- If the behavior is unintentional, then punishing the child is unwarranted and ineffective.
- Many interventions to help children are short-lasting and fail to transfer to other settings.

Rick defines the social autopsy as "the examination and inspection of a social error to determine the cause of the error, the amount of damage that occurred, and to learn about the causal factor(s) in order to prevent re-occurrence in the future. The basic principle is to assist the child in analyzing actual social errors that she has made and discuss the behavioral options that the child could have utilized in order to have improved the situation" (*It's So Much Work to Be Your Friend*, page xlix).

Rick notes that the success of the strategy is rooted in four basic steps: *practice, immediate feedback, instruction, and positive reinforcement*. He emphasizes that it is "a problem-solving technique, an opportunity for the child to participate actively in the process, is conducted by any significant adult in the child's environment (teacher, parent, bus driver), and is most effective when conducted immediately after the social event" (*It's So Much Work to Be Your Friend*, page xlix). It is not a form of punishment or an accusation or a one-time technique for teaching a social skill.

The social autopsy serves many of the goals we advocate, including (1) actively involving the child in the process in order to develop a sense of ownership and control, (2) identifying specific social problems, (3) considering different solutions for the future, and (4) attempting a solution that seems most promising.

Teaching Your Child About Thoughts,
Feelings, and Behaviors

Closely related to creating a plan with your child and the social autopsy is helping your child begin to understand how thoughts and feelings influence behavior. Obviously, the explanation offered must be in keeping with your child's cognitive and developmental level. An example we use in our book, *Angry Children, Worried Parents: Seven Steps to Help Families Manage Anger*, is also relevant in this context. Larry, a ten-year-old boy with learning disabilities, began each day in school by hitting another child. At home, when doing his homework, he shouted that his teacher didn't know how to teach and the work was dumb. As he struggled to complete his assignments, he became increasingly upset and would often rip up papers and throw things.

It was helpful for Larry to learn that engaging in schoolwork assaulted his sense of competence and elicited angry feelings and thoughts, prompting him to blame others so as to avoid feeling further humiliation. He also resorted to angry behavior as a means of expressing his frustration. Obviously, his peer relationships suffered greatly. His anger masked a very lonely, vulnerable child.

We told Larry that we could try to figure out what made him angry, what he thought about when he became angry, and how he handled these feelings (that is, his coping behaviors). Casting the issue in this nonjudgmental way helped him to join us in examining and resolving problems; in the process he began to feel a sense of control over events transpiring in his life. He showed unusual insight when he said, "I think I know why I hit other kids at school. I'd rather hit another kid and be sent to the principal's office than have to be in the classroom, where I feel like a dummy." Larry's anger was not just a response to his frustration when confronted with learning tasks, but a coping technique to remove him from the classroom. Unfortunately, this coping behavior worsened rather than improved his situation.

Given his new understanding of how feelings, thoughts, and behaviors interacted, Larry "caught himself" when frustration set in and learned to challenge the assumption that he was "dumb." This new perspective permitted him to develop more productive ways of coping, such as relating more positively to peers and requesting additional help from the teacher. In addition, as the teacher learned more about Larry's learning strengths and vulnerabilities, she was able to modify his assignments in keeping with his needs. These accommodations further reduced his frustration and anger.

Developing Strategies with Your Child

As is evident from the examples we have offered, an optimistic mindset in a child is rooted in the belief that there are adults who can help them to help themselves. When we demystify problems; when we educate children about the connections among feelings, thoughts, and behaviors and how they can begin to change all three domains; and when we teach children social skills they are lacking and how and when to apply them, we are establishing the foundation necessary for the emergence of an optimistic mindset. To nurture this optimistic mindset we must consistently and constantly engage our children in the process of solving problems.

In order to develop strategies to manage a problem, the child must agree that a problem exists. Achieving this agreement is more challenging than it may seem because many children minimize their problems and blame others. In such instances, it is essential that parents practice empathy and not attempt to extract a "confession" from their son or daughter, but rather engage them in reflecting on the situation and their response.

As Myrna Shure has highlighted through her *I Can Problem Solve* program and her books *Raising a Thinking Child* and *Raising a Thinking Preteen*, children even as young as preschool age can be engaged in the process of problem solving. We can ask children to reflect on several possible solutions to a problem and decide which one they think will work best. It is very impressive to observe the number of children who arrive at effective strategies.

Changing Negative Scripts and Mindsets

The process of considering and using new strategies to replace plans that have proved ineffective in the past demands that we as parents demonstrate the insight and courage to change our behaviors so that our children might change theirs. To use the same ineffective script repeatedly will guarantee continued frustration and anxiety. The words and behaviors we use with our children again and again in similar situations and in similar ways become the scripts of parenting. Negative scripts are saturated with words and actions that tend to increase family conflict and lead to unsatisfactory results. But when our words and actions have positive outcomes, we can consider these scripts to be productive. They deserve to be repeated.

Summary

It is not easy for parents to observe their children engaged in behaviors that demonstrate a lack of social skills or social grace. One father noted that his eight-year-old son stayed by himself even when other children were around. He said he didn't know whether to go over and hug his son or yell at him for "not even trying to make the effort to interact with kids." The father learned that a hug combined with teaching his son specific ideas about interacting with other children was a far more effective script than yelling. It also enhanced rather than depleted his son's sense of dignity and self-esteem.

Even well-intentioned parents may fall into the negative script of yelling at their children, telling their children what to do, not involving them in problem solving, and becoming frustrated and angry when attempts to ease a problem are unsuccessful. If we remain empathic and remember that children will be more willing to change their behavior when they sense our support and feel they have some control of the situation, then we will be more successful in teaching them social skills; in the process we also nurture their confidence and self-reliance.

Step 4

Employ Strategies to Improve Social Skills

As discussed in the previous Steps, you can help your child build a more effective social mindset by forging a partnership with him. Step 2 showed you how to recognize the skills your child already has and identify areas to target for improvement, and Step 3 discussed how to help your child become an active participant in the process of skill building. In this Step, we'll offer step-by-step strategies to target some specific skills that assist in developing an effective social mindset.

Building an effective social mindset requires examining and understanding thoughts, feelings, actions, and reactions, as well as developing a set of strategies and skills one can use effectively when presented with a variety of social demands. In most circumstances, we experience a thought or feeling that then guides an action or reaction. If the thoughts and feelings are positive, then we are more likely to demonstrate a positive action or reaction. If the thoughts and feelings are nega-

tive, then we are more likely to display a negative action or reaction. For many children with social skills problems, the negative actions and reactions they display in social settings are not the result of their desire to purposefully misbehave or be disliked by peers, but rather their lack of appropriate social skills to initiate or maintain a positive social interaction. For the remainder of this Step we will discuss several key social skills, ranging from back-to-basic nonverbal skills such as eye contact and body language to verbal skills such as empathy and social reciprocity.

Thinking About Thoughts and Feelings

Language is an amazing developmental skill. As children become able to express their wants, needs, and feelings through language, they also learn to use language to process and understand experiences and to modulate their behavior. This skill is the internal dialogue that can influence how we decipher, judge, and react to the world around us. For the purpose of addressing the influence of positive and negative thoughts and feelings on your child's social mindset, you must rely largely on what your child tells you about how she thinks and feels. However, as you know your child better than anyone, and actions often speak louder than words, what you observe in your child's behavior can also offer the opportunity to identify the potential thoughts and feelings influencing your child's actions and reactions.

It is important to help children learn to identify the negative thoughts and feelings that can influence their behavior. Part of your role is to help your child learn to identify and question erroneous negative attributions or assumptions and replace them with a positive, realistic evaluation of not only others' intentions but their own ability to effectively cope and participate in a variety of social opportunities.

In an attempt to target negative thoughts and feelings, we'll break negative attributions or thoughts into two categories: self versus others. Negative self-attributions include such thoughts as "I'll sound stupid if I say that" or "I'm not good at anything." Negative attributions related to the thoughts or actions of others might include "He's just asking me to play because no one else is around" or "He's ignoring me on purpose." Taken together, the thoughts and feelings about the negative attributions of either oneself or others is *negative self-talk*. Children can learn to replace negative self-talk with positive self-talk, which then can result in a more realistic interpretation of the situation and influence a more positive social interaction.

Divide a piece of paper into two columns, one entitled "Negative self-talk" and the other "Positive self-talk." Encourage your child to think about and identify a few negative self-attributions. If he has trouble, try to recall a situation in which you noticed something in his social behavior that you perceived as discomfort, lack of confidence, or even avoidance. Discuss what you observed *from your point of view* and, if needed, offer one or two suggestions of what you might have thought or felt if you had been in the same situation. Avoid pointing out mistakes or errors, and especially avoid telling your child what he should have done or needed to do. Once you and your child have identified a few negative self-thoughts, write them down in the first column.

Then encourage your child to think of and write down a positive thought that can replace the negative thought, and write it in the second column. There are three types of positive self-talk: *self-affirming thoughts, positive outcome thoughts,* and *realistic thoughts.* For example, the negative self-talk "I'm not good at anything" might be replaced with a self-affirming thought like "Maybe if I get some help and practice I'll feel better," or a positive outcome thought such as "If I do it I bet I'll have fun," or a realistic thought like "I may not be that good at soccer, but I do play baseball pretty well."

Addressing the negative attributions of others may prove more of a challenge, as there are likely times when your child does experience negative actions or reactions from others. As we'll discuss in Step 7, getting through the sometimes distressing or hurtful ups and downs of childhood and adolescence can be accomplished by not only building an effective social mindset but instilling an overall mindset of resilience, hope, and confidence. Part of an effective social mindset is to recognize when one's own thoughts and feelings regarding another's behavior can influence a change for the better in a social interaction, as well as accepting and coping with the fact that sometimes even our best efforts cannot change how other people behave or react toward us.

Although you and your child will use the same strategy to address negative attributions of others as you use to address negative self-talk, *realistic* thoughts may need to be explored further with your child in certain circumstances. For example, suppose your child repeatedly says hi to a certain child and is consistently ignored. A negative attribution in the negative self-talk column may be "He must hate me." A self-affirming thought in the positive self-talk column may be "But I have lots of friends. Maybe he didn't hear me." A positive outcome thought might be "I bet if I say it louder, then he'll hear me." Or a realistic thought might be "Maybe he's shy" or "Maybe he doesn't want to say hi back." Another realistic thought, although maybe not considered positive, might be "Maybe he doesn't want to get to know me." As you can probably recall from your childhood, sometimes friendships don't form, for whatever reason. There will be times when even a child with exceptional social skills may not "click" with certain people, or the child with whom your child is attempting to socialize may himself lack confidence or social skills. In those situations where your child may try to form a friendship but the friendship is not reciprocated, being a supportive parent and encouraging your child to stay resilient and confident is the best course of action.

Thinking About Actions and Reactions

Now that we've discussed thoughts and feelings and how to encourage your child to direct her thoughts and attributions in a more positive direction, the next step is to focus on the skills needed for positive social actions and reactions. For some children, learning back-to-basic strategies such as eye contact, body language, and tone of voice will be the initial goals. For others, learning and understanding social concepts such as empathy and reciprocity may be the major focus. It is important to note that many of these techniques and skills may take a lot of practice for some children, and to recognize that improvement (rather than complete mastery) in the targeted social skills should be considered an important and positive change. We'll now examine some guidelines for using the identified skills in the appropriate context and environment, as well as a decision-making process to identify which skills to build and which to try to reduce or eliminate. As we'll address in Step 5, everyone can fall back into old habits without commitment, conscious effort, and reminders (from ourselves and from others) of when and how to modify behavior. The next chapter will discuss how to put the target skills into a plan for practicing and reinforcing an effective social mindset.

Back to Nonverbal Basics

As identified in the Social Skills Assessment from Step 2, nonverbal skills are a very important part of the social interaction. In fact, in many cases the very beginning of the social interaction often involves physical, nonverbal skills, such as approaching an individual or a group to initiate an interaction. The following are considered basic skills, partially because they are some of the first social skills to develop. From a very early age infants display such nonverbal skills as eye contact (e.g., social gaze with their caregiver), expressive body posturing (e.g., arching back when in pain or distressed), and reciprocal facial expressions. While most children develop these skills and display them consistently, some children seem less adept with them and don't tend to use them regularly. For example, one mother of a very bright child with autism recalled that her son's lack of eye contact when she called his name was the first "red flag" she took note of when he was a toddler. Her first reaction was a concern that perhaps her son was deaf, but then she noted that he always responded to her when asked if he wanted his trains or to go for a ride in the car. In most circumstances, he responded to directions or questions by moving or doing, rather than providing eye contact or other appropriate body language to indicate he was listening to or being engaged by his caregivers.

Eye contact. This is one of the most important nonverbal skills, and it is one of the first milestones indicating social engagement of infants with their caregivers. A thrilling emotional landmark for many new parents is when their newborn focuses her gaze, even if only for a few seconds, into her parent's eyes. There is a sense of feeling connected when eyes meet, an unspoken acknowledgment of the presence and interest in another individual. As noted above, for some parents, the lack of eye contact observed in their infant or young child can trigger a sense of uneasiness or a feeling that something doesn't seem right. Many children, for whatever reason, may eventually develop this seemingly innate skill either on their own or with consistent help and support from those around them. For others, eye contact may never become an "automatic" skill and external and internal cues may be required for the long term. But, as we'll emphasize repeatedly throughout this book, if children can improve these skills and learn to practice and use them more frequently, then they will have accomplished movement toward a skill that is a hallmark of social connectedness.

If eye contact is listed on your Social Skills Target Worksheet as an area for improvement, try the following strategies:

- *Practice what you preach.* If you are talking to your child, kneel down (if needed) and look into your child's eyes. If needed, gently hold your child's chin and say "Look at my eyes."

- *Try using physical prompts as well as verbal prompts.* Using your index and middle fingers, gently and in a nonthreatening manner point to their eyes and then encourage them to track your fingers to your eyes. Put your hands on your child's shoulders to position him, gently and softly, with his shoulders in line with your shoulders and his head facing toward your face.

- *When your child is talking to you, remind her to "look at me" or "look at my eyes" as she begins talking to you.* If her gaze begins to drift away (although you don't want to encourage staring!) prompt her again, using either words or a physical gesture.

- *Catch 'em doing it.* When your child does use eye contact to indicate attention toward you, to interact with you or others, or to accompany their language, reinforce it positively and often with such statements as "Wow! Good job looking at me [or my face, or my eyes]" or "I like the way you looked at Jacob before you asked him for the toy."

- *Discuss with your child techniques or strategies you can use together to improve eye contact.* One parent described how she and her son would use the code "EB" in public places to remind him of eye contact. The code stood for "eyebrows," which he decided was a good, simple reminder to look at someone's face and eyes while in a conversation.

Body language. A picture is worth a thousand words, and in the same way, a person can convey a complex message with just the look on her face or the movement and positioning of her body. While a body posture or facial expression alone can relay a message, another important aspect of body language is how well it coordinates with verbal expression. Imagine a person with a furrowed brow and a tight-lipped mouth, with fisted hands on their hips, mumbling the phrase "Oh no, I'm not mad." The verbal statement is contradicted by the body language that says, "Oh yes, you bet I'm mad." To help your child understand and use appropriate body language, try the following strategies and techniques:

- *Encourage playing a game, like charades.* As family members display various facial expressions, have your child guess the emotion or the message they are trying to convey.

- *Have your child play a similar game.* Provide him a feeling, message, or emotion and encourage him to "act it out" without any words.

- *Provide frequent feedback about your child's facial expressions.* For example, if your child is smiling, you could say "You look like you're happy—what are you thinking about?"

- *Seek to match messages.* Point out when your child's verbal and nonverbal communication don't seem to match.

- *Practice the "mismatch" game with your messages as well.* Say one thing

but have your body "say" something else, and then discuss with your child why they didn't seem to match and what the perceived or intended message was of both the verbal and the nonverbal communication.

- *Encourage relaxation.* If needed, practice with your child physically approaching others: relaxed body posture, appropriate facial expression (smile!), appropriate distance of body space (described more below), speed of movement (some children need frequent reminders to slow it down), and good eye contact.

Personal space. All of us have likely experienced the discomfort and eventual aggravation of someone standing just a little too close behind us while waiting in line somewhere. While we attempt to make a subtle move forward, the person behind us obviously doesn't take the hint and moves up just a bit too. This behavior can easily set the tone for a less-than-positive social moment. Children, while at times less concerned with body space issues than adults, also recognize and experience discomfort when their space is continually invaded by another individual. In fact, in many cases, the "space invader's" attempts at social interaction are totally benign and not intended to cause discomfort or uneasiness with peers. If you feel that your child tends to have less awareness of personal space, try these strategies and suggestions:

- *Offer an observation.* In a nonthreatening and matter-of-fact tone, point out that your child is too close to you (or someone else) and encourage him to move back.

- *Offer physical contact.* Physically move her, guiding her gently, to a more appropriate "comfort zone," and describe it as such. A good distance when talking to acquaintances or adults is one arm's length.

- *Encourage him to take note of how others respond to him.* For example, if your child keeps telling you his friend always scoots down the bench a little bit in the lunchroom when your child tries to sit next to him, encourage a discussion about physical space and problem solving. If your child doesn't recognize it, point out that maybe he is sitting too close and his friend is trying to let him know that through his body language.

Back to Verbal Basics

There are four basic skills of verbal communication: *listening, reciprocity, timing,* and *vocal quality.* These are the most important aspects of the give-and-take in communicative exchanges. While these skills are developed (but not always implemented) by many children, some children seem to have difficulty with the flow of a normal, casual conversation. As any parent with a toddler knows, timing and listening are skills that must be encouraged and practiced to be learned. All parents, at one time or another, have had toddlers or young children (or even older children, for that matter) persistently interrupt a conversation, ignore a question, or attempt at conversation or blurt out a just-realized observation at the wrong moment.

Listening. One of the best indicators of listening ears is, ironically, eye contact. Always encourage eye contact when talking to your child. If she's in the other room, try to avoid yelling or shouting, and instead go into the room she is in and place yourself in her line of sight. Encourage her to "look at me and listen." Other strategies to address listening skills include the following:

- *Keep in mind your child's age when fostering listening skills.* Younger children have shorter attention spans, and they may also have difficulty remembering lengthy instructions or directions.

- *Try to avoid the trap of yelling to get your child to listen.* Some children tend to disregard parents' attempts at conversation or directions if they've learned they don't *really* need to pay attention until the volume goes up.

- *Provide a cue.* Before giving instructions or directions, let your child know you'll ask him to repeat what you said so you know he's listening.

- *Let her know it's OK to ask you (or someone else) to repeat something or admit she didn't hear or listen.* No one can listen to everything all the time. Reinforce the behavior if the child tells you she didn't hear (or listen) and asks for the information again.

Reciprocity. When we answer others we are *reciprocating,* or *responding.* One of the best ways to encourage your child to reciprocate a verbal communication, if it does not come naturally, is to cue or prompt. Parents must consistently (and it seems like forever sometimes) remind toddlers and young children to say "please" and "thank you" until it becomes automatic. These small but important responses are part of social and conversational reciprocity. More complex forms of reciprocity may also require frequent modeling, practice, and reminding. For example, if you ask your child about his day and he tells you, and then the conversation ceases, say, "I'd like for you to ask about my day" or "I'd like to tell you about my day." Make a statement or observation about what you would like to see happen, rather than asking a question, such as "Aren't you going to ask me about my day?" In many cases, parents might end up with an automatic, matter-of-fact "no" when they pose this question to their children! Other strategies that can be practiced and encouraged to improve reciprocity include the following:

- *Practice single sentences.* Teach your child to make one statement or ask a question when being spoken to

or when someone is attempting to converse with him.

- *Teach strategies.* Discuss with your child various aspects of conversational reciprocity, such as acknowledging a statement, accepting a compliment, providing a compliment, verbalizing an observation or a feeling, and so on.

Timing. This aspect of conversational flow can be one of the trickiest to learn and use consistently. All of us have experienced an uncomfortable silence in a conversation. A large part of timing, at least initially, is to know when to start talking. The first rule of thumb is "Don't talk while I'm talking," or the ever-popular "Please don't talk to me while I'm on the phone." More subtle aspects of timing, such as how quickly to respond to a question or when to join an existing conversation, are often best learned by observation and consistent cueing and redirection when they are not well developed. Strategies that can help teach appropriate timing include the following:

- *Model patience.* Encourage the mantra "Wait" with the child who tends to impulsively interrupt conversations. Develop a counting method of one or two seconds *after* a person finishes a sentence before responding.

- *Watch for eye contact cues.* Let your child know that if others (especially in a group) look toward her, that may be an unspoken cue that it's her turn to talk.

- *Teach rehearsal strategies.* Some children impulsively respond while others are talking because they are afraid they'll forget what they want to say. Encourage them to keep rehearsing what they want to say, and learn to say "Excuse me" or "May I interrupt" if they simply cannot wait or can't seem to get a turn in the conversation.

Vocal quality. Tone of voice, volume, inflection, cadence. While some may categorize these attributes as nonverbal because they don't relay content, we consider these traits to fall within the verbal realm simply because they are manifested only with verbal expression and can significantly influence the underlying meaning of a verbal message, just as powerfully as the nonverbal cues in the example previously discussed. For example, tone, volume, or inflection can change the message of the statement "I'm not mad," although the verbal content remains the same: "*I'm* not mad" suggests that someone, but perhaps not the person conveying the message, is mad. "I'm *not* mad" may convey that one is truly not mad. And "I'm not *mad"* gives the impression that although the speaker may not be mad, the speaker wants to convey that she does feel something.

As with some of the other skills we've discussed, the most important factor in addressing problems in vocal quality is to model, cue, remind, and provide feedback about how your child's vocal quality relays a message that is perhaps different from the actual language in the message. Many children need frequent reminders about appropriate volume, which parents often refer to as using "an indoor voice." It is important to note, however, that if you have tried providing reminders and cues and your child's vocal quality continues to be significantly different or unusual, consultation with your child's pediatrician to rule out potential physical causes (such as hearing loss or irregularities of the palate, tongue, or vocal chord) is recommended.

Summary

Now that we've discussed some specific strategies to address thoughts, feelings, actions, and reactions, we'll discuss in Step 5 how to start getting involved and practicing not only the skills described in Step 4 while keeping in mind the goals laid out in Step 3. As noted in the previous Steps, building an effective social mindset requires not only adding to the arsenal of appropriate social skills but also helping your child become an active participant in the process. Fostering an optimistic mindset, developing empathy, and demystifying social skill problems will also continually evolve as social skills are practiced, modeled, and learned initially in a safe environment as well as in the real world with peers and other adults.

Step 5

Practice Social Interactions

Now that we've discussed some of the skills helpful in building an effective social mindset and improving social skills, let's talk about how and when to use these skills in certain contexts or environments. As we've noted, all children will have some effective social skills in their repertoire, and you should continue to use these well-developed skills while building and practicing the social skills targeted for improvement in Step 2. An effective social mindset requires not just an array of social skills, but the ability to decipher when, why, and how to implement these skills in social settings and when a change is needed.

When

The question of when to start a social interaction can be answered by looking at two main factors: *setting* and *interpersonal timing*. Many children choose to start interacting in the wrong setting, resulting in discomfort from peers and disapproval from adults. I (Kristy Hagar) once worked with a young girl who was described by all as a social butterfly. She enjoyed and frequently sought out social interactions with others. Although she seemed to have and use a variety of social skills (she approached others comfortably, had good eye contact and a friendly smile, and was always able to think of a conversation-starter), her parents had been getting increasingly frequent reports from school that she was disruptive in class. She sometimes interrupted the teacher during lectures or instructions. Other children started to request to sit at different tables because she often interrupted them during their work. This young lady had difficulty determining the setting in which it was or was not appropriate to start interacting with others.

The other major factor related to the "when" of interacting was described in Step 4: the *interpersonal timing* of entering an ongoing conversation or starting a conversation. Some children

attempt to interact by barging into an ongoing conversation or interrupting someone at an inopportune time. In addition to the strategies described in Step 4 related to timing, encourage your child to explore the following questions to assist with determining the "when" of getting involved:

- *Is it OK to talk in the place I am right now?* For example, churches, classrooms, and movie theaters are places this question should be asked.

- *Is anything happening in the place I'm in right now that would be disrupted if I start talking?* Is someone else talking or doing something?

- *Is it OK to say something now, or do I need to wait?* Once I've assessed the place and the people, is it the right time to talk?

- *Is the person I want to talk to doing anything right now?*

- *If I say the person's name, does he look up at me?*

- *Should I or can I ask, "Can I talk to you now?"*

Why

The three main reasons to interact that are related to an effective social mindset are *to express a thought or feeling, to initiate an action,* or *to respond with a reaction.* When attempting to help your child identify some of the whys of a social interaction, encourage the following questions:

1. *Do I want to tell someone how I'm feeling or what I'm thinking?*

2. *Do I want to ask someone to do something or get involved with a person or a group?*

3. *Do I want to say or do something in response to someone else?*

Although these seem like very basic questions, in many settings answering yes to any of them can help guide your child in making the next choice of *how* to get involved.

How

Now that we've targeted the skills for improving your child's social mindset and discussed whens and whys of social interaction, the next step is to determine *how* to practice building these skills in a variety of settings. Refer back to the Social Skills Target Worksheet in Step 2. This sheet can be used to help keep track of not only the skills your child already possesses and implements on a daily basis, but also the skills that are targeted for strengthening or improving. As one skill is introduced and eventually well learned and used, another skill can be targeted to add to a growing repertoire of skills reflecting an effective social mindset.

Practice Makes Perfect

As parents, we assume multiple roles in interacting with our children. We are nurturers, protectors, coaches, and providers for our children. We are also role models, and our children tend to display our traits and skills (either purposefully or accidentally). Your role is not just to coach your child in building effective social skills, but also to model the appropriate behaviors and set up situations that allow for comfortable practice and feedback. Without question, the best environment to start building your child's social skills is in your home. Home is a safe and predictable environment where parents and siblings can serve as familiar coaches and role models to help develop the child's skills.

Practicing in the Family

Begin working with the first skill targeted on the Social Skills Target Worksheet, as well as one or two of the successful social skills your child possesses and often demonstrates. Next, identify two or three situations or settings in the home environment that can set the stage for using your child's social strengths while also working on the targeted skill. For example, if eye contact is a skill to build, skill-building opportunities at home can include eating at the dinner table or playing a game with parents and siblings. If sharing is the targeted skill, then the skill-building times could include play activities such as coloring or drawing (setting up the situation where all the children share the materials), helping with a fun activity (such as sharing the task of making cookies), or doing chores (for example, sharing time with the vacuum cleaner or duster).

Following is a list of home-based activities that can serve as skill-building opportunities:

- Eating at the table
- Doing chores
- Playing games
- Arts and crafts
- Cooking
- Playing outside
- Doing homework
- Computer time
- Cooperative or multiple-player video games
- Learning or sharing a hobby
- Reading

Once the setting *(when)* is right for the social interaction and the targeted skills have been discussed *(how)*, help set the skills in motion by discussing the *why* of the social interaction. For some children, it may be helpful to provide consistent, reflective feedback of what you think their thoughts and feelings might be ("You're smiling—it looks like you're enjoying this game") and describe how to initiate interactions ("You look like maybe you want to play the game with us. Do you want to join in?") or reactions ("John asked if you wanted to play; do you think you'd like to tell him 'Yes' and join in?").

The most common and supportive resource within the family, other than the parents, is siblings. It is important (and practical) to enlist siblings' participation in the skill-building exercises. With some preparation and guidance, siblings younger or older can contribute to the process, resulting in a positive learning experience for both the child learning to practice his skills and his siblings.

When setting up situations at home, let your child know that you'd like to enlist her siblings in working on the targeted skills. Depending on your child's age and personality, she may be comfortable with this, have a few minor reservations, or be totally appalled that her siblings are going to know about this plan of action. Some children, understandably, feel uncomfortable and possibly embarrassed that they are having to "work" on skills that may seem much more natural and effortless for their siblings or peers. If your child resists or is hesitant, try to discuss the concerns and develop a compromise. When discussing with the child's siblings the supportive role you'd like them to play, keep the following guidelines in mind:

- Be as discreet as possible to protect your child's feelings.

- Encourage the siblings to be supportive and not tease or criticize.

- Outline specific things they can do to help, as well as specific things that are not helpful or supportive.

- Acknowledge their attempts to help and their appropriate social behaviors.

- Avoid comparing the skills that a sibling possesses and uses well with those of the child working on her skills.

Practicing in the "Real World"

Once targeted skills have been practiced and supported in the home environment, the next step is to try to practice them in other familiar and supportive settings. For many children, school is the next logical setting for practice. As with the home environment, the school environment also requires a coach to help set up situations in which the child can succeed and to model and reinforce the appropriate behaviors. In most circumstances, your child's teacher is a natural choice to serve as the role model and support person for encouraging social skills in the school environment. Encourage your child to discuss his skill-building goals with the teacher or other school personnel. Involving school personnel will likely be easier if your child is in elementary school. Junior high or high school teachers are often more difficult to enlist due to the fact that they have so many more students and have a limited amount of time during the day with each student. Additionally, teenagers may be much more hesitant to discuss their difficulties and enlist other people's help, but it can be done.

Enlisting the teacher's help. This book includes an appendix for educators that you can share with your child's teacher as a first step in approaching the teacher about enlisting his help in the school setting. In most circumstances, the social skills learned and practiced at home will benefit from reinforcement and practice at school. Teachers or other adults working with your child may already have provided important feedback about the improvements they've seen in your child's skills as you've been practicing them at home. Support from your child's teachers can foster the continued improvement of your child's social skills in a setting that is often much more demanding of these skills than the home environment.

Let your child know what you'd like to do, and try to get her blessing and (ideally) participation. Set up a meeting with your child's teacher and bring a copy of the appendix for educators (pages 83-89) and the Social Skills Target Worksheet identifying the skills that have been targeted at home (page 27). Bring the teacher a copy of the blank Social Skills Assessment (page 26) and ask her to complete it describing what she sees as your child's social strengths and weaknesses in the classroom setting. In many cases, the goals may be the same, such as improved eye contact or refraining from invading others' personal space. If the concerns are different, try to pick one or two that generally fit what you've been working on at home so that your child has consistent goals to work on with consistent feedback about a similar targeted behavior in home and school settings. Remember

to focus on one or two specific skills at a time rather than overloading and potentially frustrating your child by targeting too many different skills at once.

Once everyone has agreed on the targeted skills, a daily feedback sheet that can be used to keep track of your child's progress toward his goals can be helpful. Older children (age eight and up) should be encouraged to keep their feedback sheet and monitor their performance. The teacher should review it periodically throughout the day (or after targeted settings such as recess or lunch) and at the end of the day for comments and suggestions. For younger children, the teacher should keep track of the feedback sheet throughout the day and then place it with other school papers for the return home. Consider using a spiral-bound notebook to keep track of the social skill targets and goals. An example of a school-based worksheet appears on the next page.

Enlisting other adults' help. As your child continues to feel a sense of success and accomplishment in the home and school settings, it will be important to continue to foster and reinforce social skills in a variety of other settings. As your child develops an effective social mindset, other adults and peers will be increasingly present and influential in the development, reinforcement, and adaptation of your child's social skills. Your child's involvement in activities outside of the school and home settings can be considered and tried when both you and your child feel the time is right.

Extracurricular activities can provide an excellent opportunity to build social skills and develop a sense of pride and accomplishment in a hobby, sport, or activity. When deciding whether to involve a coach, teacher, or team leader that your child may be involved with, discuss the pros

Sample Social Skills Worksheet

Name _____ Date _____

My goals	My teacher will remind me	Check times
1.Use eye contact when talking to others or being spoken to.	She'll use the phrase "Look at my eyes." She'll tap my shoulder if I'm talking to someone and I'm not looking at the person I'm talking to.	10:00 AM 11:00 AM Lunch 1:00 PM 2:00 PM
2. Keeping an elbow's-length space from my friends in class and at the lunch table.	She'll use the phrase "elbow room." She'll remind me if I need to move my chair back.	10:30 Center 11:15 Center Lunch 2:00 Music 2:50 Art Table

and cons with your child. Explore the concerns both you and your child may have, such as perhaps feeling "singled out" or conveying to an unfamiliar adult the social difficulties your child has experienced.

When your child is enrolled in a new activity, adopting a "wait and see" attitude may be best before attempting to enlist other adults. If you and your child feel confident that any mild social concerns or difficulties can be handled without involving other adults, and your experiences continue to confirm that feeling, then this could be a successful approach and should be considered a job well done in developing an effective social mindset. If, however, problems arise, then discussing your child's social skills and her comfort in social situations with the adults working with her should be considered. This would be especially important if the alternative, in either your child's mind or yours, is to abandon an activity that your child was really looking forward to.

If you and your child decide to discuss your child's social difficulties with other adults, emphasize at the beginning your request for confidentiality. Also, don't assume that the adult will automatically think this is a sensitive issue or important concern for your child. Many experienced teachers or leaders in the community have probably seen many children with mild social or performance difficulties and been able to coax them to a level of comfort and participation. If you attempt to discuss your child's social skills goals and request proactive encouragement and support from your child's coaches, team leaders, or teachers but feel they do not seem interested or invested in assisting your child, then you and your child need to reconsider your child's participation in that activity.

If, on the other hand, you have a concerned adult willing to help your child along, share with them the goals you and your child have set. Discuss your child's social strengths, as well as the goals achieved and the goals still to be mastered.

While it may be unrealistic to ask a coach, gym teacher, or leader to keep a written feedback sheet, they can often keep mental notes of your child's behavior and reinforce the settings and situations in which your child can practice his skills. Additionally, it can be helpful to try to get some quick verbal feedback following the activity or event, then discuss the feedback with your child on the way home. Again, reinforcing your child's attempts and conscious efforts to improve her social skills should be discussed and encouraged across settings.

Summary

This step has provided a framework for taking the skills described in Step 4 and practicing them at home and in other settings. We discussed the importance of understanding the when, why, and how of an effective social mindset and provided suggestions for setting the stage in the home setting to start working on these skills. We outlined steps for enlisting the school's help and practicing these skills in the school setting as you and your child become more comfortable with an increasing repertoire of skills. Finally, we discussed ways to determine whether and how to involve other adults in other settings.

In Step 6, we'll discuss some common problems that can arise as you and your child start to work on the goals, and Step 7 will provide additional information about fostering resilience, hope, and confidence as part of an overall effective mindset for success in social settings and in life.

Step 6

Assess and Solve Problems

Once you have identified your child's social skills problems, created a plan to develop key skills, and begun your journey, it would be ideal if the course were straight and free of obstacles. However, this is rarely the case. You can be sure that obstacles will arise that will interfere with the effectiveness of your plan. The more you are aware of these possible roadblocks to success, the better prepared you can be to minimize or avoid them. In this Step we will review many common obstacles and how to overcome them.

Challenged Parenting

As parent trainer and author Sharon Weiss points out, there is no better example of the proverbial emotional roller coaster than raising children. Feeling tired or overwhelmed one day can cause you to mismanage a conflict, and what seems like a challenge one day may not seem so bad the next. But even if you have fleeting moments where you feel successful, if the same social skills problems occur day after day despite your best efforts to improve them, you are a *challenged parent*. You may fear that your child's struggles are seen by others as a measure of your competency as a parent or person. Feeling this way can translate to reactive anger management and negative scripts in the face of problems.

Sometimes children seem challenging because you compare them with other children, typically siblings or peers. They may also be challenging because their temperament simply is not a good match with yours. In addition, the truly challenging child evokes a sense of desperation. As you attempt to better understand and, in this case, develop social skills, the challenging child stymies parental attempts to change adverse behavior. The challenging child is not just a child with a label, but a child who may have outstripped your ability to help him. This might make you feel paralyzed, and frustrated to hear yourself reacting in the same ineffective way again and again. Sometimes you do nothing and let it go. Then one day you are terribly concerned that your child spends almost all of his free time in isolated activities. Don't be surprised at your reactions. Your emotions prove you are normal. You obviously love your child, but the frustration that comes from feeling impotent can and does further impede your relationship with your child.

Change Starts With You

Although you are not the cause of your child's social skills problems, you are part of the solution. Change in your child's behavior starts with you. Each new conflict is a teachable moment. What is your child learning from you? Is the current situation an example of not one but two people who lack effective strategies? The emotions you show, the behaviors you demonstrate, and the words you choose to express yourself are all models. Children don't necessarily do what we say, but they do what we do. It is your responsibility to set a good example.

In addition to modeling the behaviors you want your child to emulate, you can make a consistent effort to offer alternative behaviors for social skills and the expression of emotions. It is important to communicate with your child ways that she can appropriately say to you and to others, "I disagree." These might include saying, "This stinks" but not include saying, "You stink." You should also make clear to your child that when receiving directions, she may ask for a reason in a calm tone or seek clarification. You

must know what you think is acceptable and communicate it clearly to your child.

Change Takes Time

Unrealistic expectations are one of the biggest obstacles to change. Expecting too much regarding the kinds of changes you will see, how long they will last, or how quickly they will take place is likely to distort your definition of progress. The acquisition of effective social skills is gradual, and your expectations for your child's progress must reflect this understanding. For example, if your child is disrespectful, it is unrealistic to expect that any instruction or technique will result in his suddenly acting perfectly politely overnight. But if the frequency of disrespectful comments decreases from three a day to two a day, that is progress. The expectation is not that your child will never talk back or that he will always respond respectfully. The terms *never* and *always* do not apply to behavior. Behavior does not occur in absolutes, and expecting it to will only increase frustration. If you wait for perfection, you will be missing many opportunities to savor and praise improvement. If you don't notice small changes you won't see progress—and progress is success. Progress is measured in steps. It does not happen all at once and it does not happen overnight.

It is important to be prepared for frequent setbacks. Just when you think your child has mastered the skills necessary to initiate and maintain a social interaction, something will go wrong. When positive change occurs, and it will, know now that whatever is going right may not last. The best behavioral changes, like the worst, invariably pass. If you anticipate these lapses you will be less frustrated when they happen.

Realistic expectations of inevitable setbacks will reduce your frustration and anger as well as your child's.

When improvement occurs, some parents fail to recognize it and others assume it signals a cure. When the inevitable regression happens, parents and children are more disappointed than if no change had occurred at all. Inflated expectations result in increased frustration despite improvement. It is essential to narrow your focus, define changes in terms of improvement and not perfection, anticipate ups and downs, and reinforce even small successes.

Power Struggles

Power struggles between parents and children can occur over just about anything, so it's wise to anticipate the possibility that they will occur as you practice your plan to help your child learn, develop, and use new social skills. Ordinary disputes become power struggles when both parties become entrenched, determined not to yield. Often, both sides lose perspective, and typically parents and children engaged in these struggles say and do things that are hurtful and counterproductive. Whichever side prevails, the outcome is never worth the destructive process.

As the parent, it is your responsibility to prevent power struggles to the extent possible and to resolve any that can't be prevented as you attempt to help your child develop social skills. Effective anger management on your part may be the key factor that minimizes the frequency of power struggles between you and your child. In a previous book in our series, *Angry Children, Worried Parents*, we offered a set of six guidelines to avoid power struggles:

1. *Ignore minor resistance or misbehavior.* Pick your battles carefully. You can't work on everything at one time.

2. *Don't badger or criticize.* Remember, if your child were capable of developing efficient and effective social skills independently, she would do so. Even a single sarcastic remark uttered out of frustration is likely to increase anger and animosity and could possibly provoke a power struggle.

3. *Avoid nagging, lecturing, and arguing.* These strategies are ineffective. Children typically don't listen to parental words of wisdom, much less a sermon. If your child argues, state your position calmly and walk away. If you are not there, there is no one he can argue with. At a later point you can return to the activity.

4. *Get out of the moment.* Try to see the situation in the context of the big picture. Ask yourself if this one point is worth the toll the argument may take on your relationship with your child and your ability to help your child develop effective social interaction. Will an intractable approach further her understanding of the point you are trying to make? Can whatever you have to say wait until later? Can you express yourself in a constructive, nonthreatening, rational way?

5. *Plan ahead.* A good way to reduce the frequency of power struggles is to have a plan for early recognition and intervention. This applies not just

to social skills but to all areas of family life. With your child, list on paper the situations or issues that trigger power struggles. Develop a structure for handling them. Under what circumstances can bedtime change? What is the policy for a last-minute request to have a friend spend the night, particularly if such sleepovers are rare occurrences? Think about these situations and plan for them ahead of time, not when you and your child are in a heated argument. Once you have determined procedures, discuss them with your child and the rest of the family. Let everyone know what the outcomes will be when these situations are resolved smoothly and when they are not.

6. *Create strategies to disagree.* Agree on ways for you and your child to disagree. Even young children should be afforded the opportunity to express their opinions, including anger, frustration, or disappointment, without triggering a negative response from parents. Your child is guaranteed to feel all these emotions at some point. Notice acceptable ways he already uses to express his feelings. Suggest methods for your child to say "I think that is not a good idea" without your immediately becoming defensive. Remember, there is little chance of raising a child without disagreement.

No one wins in a power struggle. If you think you are in a power struggle you probably are, and because there can be no winner, the only solution is to disengage.

Unclear Expectations

Your goal is planned and responsive parenting rather than reactive parenting as you attempt to help your child develop effective social skills. Arguing, blaming, and agonizing will not result in clear thinking, meaningful changes in your behavior, or advanced planning for the next time.

All children need limits. Consistently enforced, clearly stated guidelines give a sense of security and predictability. If your child knows in advance what is expected and what the consequences are of meeting or not meeting those expectations, then the outcome is the child's choice. Too often, parents communicate rules to children only after they are broken. This "after-the-fact parenting" is not only ineffective but can lead to increased problems. Telling a child he should have known better when social problems occur is not likely to lead to effective change.

It is easier for your child to remember rules she helps develop, and it is easier for her to stay focused on behaviors she thinks are important. So get her input: Ask what she thinks she needs to work on and help her set a few goals. (Fewer is better.) If your child is a part of the solution she is less likely to feel as if she is the brunt or cause of problems.

Rules do not in and of themselves prevent negative behavior. Many parents develop a rule to cover every situation, and attempt to teach social skills in a similar fashion. However, creating too many rules in an effort to control or change behavior frustrates children and defeats parents. This kind of overcontrol makes it impossible to monitor behavior and enforce rules consistently, and often leads to rebellion. Your child will not remember what you said this morning, let alone what you said yesterday. If you assign yourself the responsibility of praising your child every day for each rule followed, particularly in social situations, you will quickly narrow your list. If the rule is important, it warrants praise. Rules are one area where the maxim less is more applies.

Excuses and Avoidance

Parents whose children are struggling often overprotect them, fearing that the child is incapable of handling the situation. But social skills problems will not disappear on their own; they must be faced lest they become more intense and debilitating. Making excuses for your child or allowing him to avoid certain situations, while motivated by love and concern, may actually maintain his problems. If an intervention strategy is ineffective, the alternative is not to permit your child to avoid that situation but rather to face it equipped with a new strategy. When children learn to avoid difficult situations, the relief that they find is temporary and only furthers additional avoidance.

Too Much Reassurance

Parents can sometimes offer too much reassurance in their efforts to pave the path of socialization with success. Offering reassurance is appropriate as long as it is realistic and does not minimize or invalidate the child's struggles, emotions, and perceptions. However, too much reassurance can make children feel as if their parents are not listening to them or do not appreciate the emotional pain they may be experiencing. In particular, children with social anxiety often feel overwhelmed and are not easily comforted by comments of a challenging or dismissing nature. For the socially anxious child, every fear is very real and not easily assuaged. As a parent, you must balance validation of your child's worries with realistic appraisal of those worries. This balance can be strengthened when children are involved in a discussion of what would help them to cope with their worries.

Being Too Directive

Parents may be too directive when planning and implementing strategies. It is vital to avoid the trap of telling children what to do, especially when children are passive in their participation or when you are stressed and frustrated. Be calm and firm in the face of passivity or your child's fear, but do not tell her what to do. Remember that a major component of resilience, a vital skill you want to help your child develop, is a feeling of control over one's life. That feeling is reinforced in your child when she believes she has contributed to the solution to her problems.

If your child is extremely passive or anxious in the problem-solving process, it may be appropriate initially for you to suggest possible solutions as a way of highlighting that solutions exist and then to engage the child in a discussion of which solution feels most comfortable and which is most likely to succeed. The offering of choices could be done with all strategies. When the child makes a decision, you can highlight the child's involvement by saying, "That sounds like a good choice; let's try it and see what happens."

Making such comments reinforces a sense of ownership and is one of the most effective strategies when children are passive in the solution-generating process.

Becoming Impatient

All parents would like their child's social skills to improve as quickly as possible. It is painful to observe children in distress. However, as we observed in previous Steps, what appears to be a solid plan of action may prove to be ineffective or may not result in a positive outcome as quickly as desired. If you are not emotionally prepared for this possible occurrence, you can easily become frustrated with yourself and your child. It is important to establish realistic goals for progress and to review obstacles as positive learning experiences rather than frustrating and defeating setbacks.

When Your Child Is Passive

It is immensely frustrating for parents to feel they are doing all the work, whether it's setting up play dates or reminding a child to do homework. Some children are just naturally passive. For others, passivity may be the result of a particular worry, such as fear that a play date may not go well. For still other children, passivity may be the result of past social failures or humiliation. Many children in such circumstances quickly decide the easiest way to avoid future failure and humiliation is to simply avoid future social contact. If your child is particularly passive in this process, listen closely and try to learn the source of the passivity. Is it temperamental? Is it coping strategy? Or is it simply lack of effective social skills?

Once you understand the source of passivity, patiently involve your child in setting goals. Don't be afraid to be a bit more directive. Create a timetable and develop at least one or two backup plans to implement if the first plan meets with limited success. Avoid reinforcing passive behavior by continuing to measure positive change. Even small steps represent success, and they should be acknowledged.

When Your Child Is Excessively Worried or Fearful

Some children are extremely anxious in social situations. It is important for you to recognize, acknowledge, and respond to these patterns of temperament by adjusting your expectations. Extreme social anxiety typically presents as avoidance or excessive isolation. This pattern may be true for depressed children as well. A key step for you is to distinguish whether your child at one time was socializing effectively and has since regressed, or has never socialized. In the former case, seek out professional help to understand the forces that may be shaping your child's current social interactions. In the latter case, be patient. If you suspect that a significant level of worry or hopeless or helpless thinking is playing a role, seek professional help.

When your child seems to isolate himself, even in the face of social opportunity, consider limiting the number of peers during a play session. Focus on one-on-one interactions. Be directive in planning an activity. Plan activities that initially require less face-to-face discussion and more shared or parallel enjoyment, such as taking a trip to the park rather than playing a board game. It is important to remember that some children who isolate socially are shy. They feel inadequate and incompetent and tend to elicit few positive social responses from peers. They are often nontalkative and socially inactive. Socially withdrawn or isolated children generally have few strategies available for solving social problems and tend to lack persistence in their attempts to resolve those problems. In some situations, though, they can display socially active behavior. If this is the case, your child is capable but lacks consistent, predictable, and independent capability to demonstrate these behaviors on a regular basis.

Some children display social learning disability. These children have difficulty taking the perspective of others. They often struggle to understand how others' thoughts, feelings, or motivations. Social learning problems are closely associated with autism and Asperger's syndrome. This book provides helpful strategies for children with social learning problems, but it is important that you have your child evaluated by a professional and that you understand the nature of your child's social learning problems. As with teaching a poorly coordinated child to ride a bicycle, children with social learning disability often progress at very slow rates.

When Global Developmental Impairments Lead to Social Immaturity

It is often the case that children's social skills are generally equivalent to their intellectual skills, but not always. Thus, sometimes some very bright children struggle to successfully interact socially while some children with low intellectual ability socialize well. However, when children's developmental functioning and rate of growth is dramatically slow, they often fall far enough behind to be considered developmentally delayed. Children with weaker intellectual skills often are interested in playmates and play activities at a level consistent with their functioning rather than their chronological age. In these cases it is important for you to work with a professional to understand your child's rate of development and current level of maturity. Then you can seek out younger peers and avoid intellectually overwhelming activities. In these circumstances, most important, it is essential that you accept and understand your child's developmental level.

When Children Are Impulsive

Friendships are developed and maintained through play. Because of their inattentive, hyperactive patterns of behavior, impulsive children may be deprived of successful interactions at young ages and thus fail to begin to take the steps necessary for appropriate social development. Other children quickly become aware of the impulsive child's behavior and view this child negatively. This often leads to rejection, which frequently fosters even more problems. The frustration of being rejected can result in an increase of aggressive and coercive attempts to control friends.

In many research studies, impulsive children are identified as socially isolated and disliked. These children understand what to do, but their impulsive temperament makes it difficult for them to do what they know. In particular, impulsive children struggle with a number of specific social skills. They often do not know how to engage in rough play appropriately. They don't make very many positive statements toward others (such as saying, "I like the way you did that") or appropriate verbal requests (for example, saying, "Please pass me the crayon" instead of "Give me that"). Keep these specific social skills in mind as you evaluate problems your impulsive child may be experiencing. It is also likely that as a result of their impulsive, inattentive, and hyperactive behavior they may not learn how to take the perspective of others or label emotions effectively. This may interfere with social maturation.

The plan for helping your impulsive, socially inefficient child must include plenty of opportunities for generalization and success. Impulsive children will require many social skills practice opportunities in the real world if they are to develop efficient social skills. If your child's problems are sufficient to warrant a diagnosis of and medical treatment for attention deficit hyperactivity disorder, you may also discover a significant improvement in your child's social interaction when treatment is initiated. However, it is important to keep in mind that pills will not substitute for skills. Many children with ADHD, even when treated medically, continue to experience some degree of social problems.

When Language and Learning Problems Impair Socialization

Children with language and perceptual motor problems struggle academically and, in many cases, socially. Again, it is important for you to understand your child's developmental strengths and weaknesses. Avoid setting up your child for failure in social situations in which their language or nonverbal comprehension abilities may be limited.

When Children Are Aggressive

Common traits of socially aggressive children include verbal and physical assault, teasing, provoking, quarreling, and fighting, typically as methods of conflict resolution. Aggressive children tend to ignore and violate the rights of others through the use of physical, emotional, or psychological force. Though their tactics may be effective, they are typically inappropriate and tend to generate many negative side effects. Such children are often rejected by peers. They are at risk during their adolescent years for discipline and juvenile justice problems.

If your child exhibits socially aggressive behavior, keep in mind that although they may be able to do what they know, they are often impulsively prone to respond aggressively to social problems. Typically, they also exhibit few prosocial behaviors such as helping, sharing, or cooperating. They tend to use threats, aggression, or destruction to meet their needs. Because this pattern of behavior is powerfully predictive of later adolescent and possibly adult problems, it is important for you to be aware of and target them. Often, professional help is necessary.

It has also been found that aggressive boys actually display faulty social attribution and limited problem-solving capability. That is, they tend to attribute their misfortunes to the hostile behaviors of peers. They interpret social cues from peers as signs of hostility and they infer hostile intentions even in ambiguous situations. Their problem-solving strategies tend to be less effective, less specific, and more aggressive than those of their socially skilled peers. They appear to perceive fewer options to resolve conflicts and tend to offer aggressive strategies rather than cooperation, assertion, or other prosocial alternatives. They have a tendency to defy interpersonal goals and thus endorse coercive, disruptive solutions to social problems. In sum, then, they appear to be deficient at generating competent, nonaggressive solutions and are biased toward endorsing aggressive solutions. This pattern of behavior must be targeted if aggressive children are to develop more efficient and effective social and interpersonal skills.

Not Knowing When More Is Needed

While we emphasize perseverance and backup plans, we also believe that you must recognize when the original plan and backup strategies are ineffective. Your timetable to determine effectiveness of a particular strategy is in part determined by the level of problems your child experiences in daily functioning. However, a point may be reached in which you will exhaust your resources. In such situations, professional help is often necessary. Although parents feel that they should be all things to their children, being a loving, effective parent does not mean you can solve every one of your child's problems. Rather,

it implies that you know when you need support and the input of professionals, and that despite your struggles you remain connected to and supportive of your child.

Summary

This Step provided you with information to assist with problems that may arise as you and your child start to develop an effective social mindset and build successful social skills. We discussed some of the common behaviors that parents tend to fall back on when their own expectations are higher than the actual change or improvement that is taking place. We explored several of the factors that can lead to social skill problems that were described in Step 2 and provided a framework for coping with these issues.

Finally, we want to reiterate that there may be times when professional assistance is needed. In the next, final step, we will discuss an important aspect that is essential for not only effective social skills but for the overall well-being of any child: a resilient mindset.

Step 7

Nurture a Resilient Mindset in Your Child

The dreams and wishes we have for our children include success in school, satisfaction in their lives, friendships, and the ability to become a functional member of their community. To realize these goals children must learn social skills that permit them to relate comfortably and compassionately toward others. They must also possess the inner strength to deal successfully day after day with the challenges and demands they face. This ability to cope, feel competent, and overcome problems is called *resilience*.

Resilient children are able to deal with stress and pressure. They bounce back from disappointments or adversity. They are capable of setting goals, solving problems, and acting responsibly. The skills that make up a resilient mindset explain why some children overcome great obstacles while others become victims of the stresses and challenges they encounter.

Regardless of our ethical, cultural, religious, or scientific beliefs, the development of a resil-

ient mindset in our children is an essential parenting task. The child who has a resilient mindset carries a set of tools to deal with any problems he faces in everyday life. Children with social skills problems fare better when they learn strategies to foster a resilient mindset to accompany their social mindset. The concept of resilience is in part defined by a process of parenting that instills in children a mindset to seek and find satisfaction and happiness. Each interaction with our children provides an opportunity to help them weave a strong and resilient personal fabric.

Resilient children possess a view of the world that enables them to meet challenges and pressures. They can translate this view into effective action. Resilient youngsters are hopeful and possess high self-worth. They feel special and appreciated. They have learned to set realistic goals and expectations for themselves. They are capable of solving problems and making good decisions. They view mistakes as challenges to confront rather than stresses to avoid. They have developed the interpersonal skills to deal successfully with peers and adults.

These qualities, however, are not acquired from a pill or a class. Rather, they are nurtured by parents who possess an understanding of important principles, ideas, and actions that contribute to the formation of a resilient mindset in their children. In Step 7 we provide strategies and guidelines to help your children develop five important qualities of resilience. We will introduce each quality and then offer several strategies and suggestions for you to consider in your day-in and day-out parenting. We believe that by using these strategies with children with social skills problems, you can strengthen their resolve and ability to benefit from your help.

Making Children Feel Special and Appreciated

When children feel loved and accepted they also feel special and appreciated. They believe they hold a special place in the hearts and minds of their parents. They sense that their parents truly enjoy being with them. In this way, parents can serve as *charismatic adults* in the lives of their children. The late psychologist Dr. Julius Segal introduced this term to describe adults who, in their interactions with children, convey love, acceptance, and support, qualities that help children feel unconditional love. This foundation is critical because it allows children to be less defensive and more receptive to learning from parents. Ensuring that your child feels loved and appreciated is a cornerstone of helping her develop a resilient mindset. It is little wonder that adults who have overcome great childhood adversity often attribute their success to at least one

adult who was present for them during challenging times in their childhood and adolescent years.

Every interaction with your child is an opportunity to help him feel loved and appreciated. In some situations, such as when you are frustrated and angry with your child, this is more difficult to accomplish, but those are the very situations in which it is most vital to reinforce a resilient mindset. Here are six strategies to help you in this process.

1. *Let your memories of childhood be your guide.* Incorporate into your parenting practices those experiences that helped you feel loved, and avoid those that did not. Strive to avoid saying or doing things that led you to feel less worthy, less loved, more alone, and more angry as a child and, in many cases, as an adult.

2. *Create traditions and special times.* Creating traditions and setting aside special time with your children each day, week, or month establishes an atmosphere in which they feel loved. In doing so you convey the message to them that they are important to you and you enjoy being with them.

3. *Don't miss significant occasions.* If we are not present for the important events in our children's lives, they are likely to feel unimportant. Time spent with them, particularly during special events, pays future dividends in the time they will invest in us as adults, allowing us to share in their adult lives as well.

4. *Be demonstrative with your love.* Although some parents find it diffi-

cult to display affection, we must all strive to let our children know they are loved on a daily basis.

5. *Build up your children.* As parents we routinely engage in a chipping-away process without realizing it. We correct rather than teach, and in doing so, we erode or fail to reinforce the features of a resilient mindset. It is difficult to develop a sense of self-worth, security, and confidence in the presence of people who are unappreciative.

6. *Accept your children.* A major challenge of parenting is accepting children for who they are and not what we want them to be. The best way to help children learn social skills and social grace is to create an atmosphere in which they feel safe and secure. In such a climate they are able to recognize that what we are attempting to teach them is based firmly on our unconditional love.

Loving Unconditionally

This last point deserves to be highlighted further. To nurture a resilient mindset requires that we love and accept our children unconditionally. Keep in mind that the concepts of fairness and acceptance are not synonymous with treating each child the same or having the same expectations and goals for each child. Fairness is demonstrated by responding to each child based on the child's particular temperament and needs. This type of acceptance is a foundation of resilience. Acceptance is rooted in unconditional love and provides an environment for the reinforcement of a resilient mindset. When children feel accepted they are more likely to be secure and confident, particularly in facing challenges and adversities.

A basic premise of this book is the acceptance by parents that some children come into the world more likely to have difficulty developing social skills. As children grow, differences in abilities are manifested in the ways they learn, the activities they choose, their ease in dealing with daily life, and their success relating with peers and adults. We must avoid falling into the trap of telling our children we accept them, but . . . that is, we accept them, but only if they behave or achieve in certain ways. This represents *conditional* love. Acceptance must serve as the link between our love and the process of defining realistic and obtainable goals with our children. Here are four strategies to help in the acceptance process.

1. *Become educated.* The key to your effort is to become familiar with your children's temperament, development, and behavior and use this information proactively in planning parenting practices and helping them develop social skills. By understanding and accepting the unique qualities of each child we can best assist in fostering a resilient mindset.

2. *Measure your mindset.* Honestly consider your reactions in the past to your children's feelings and behavior. In Step 3 we discussed the importance of empathy in helping children begin to deal with their problems. Make certain that you always begin with empathy.

3. *Make necessary adjustments.* If there is a good match between your expectations and what your children can do, you stand the best chance of helping them deal constructively with their interpersonal relations. Don't give up your dreams and wishes, but realistically understand your children's current state and help them work from that point. Separate the dreams you have for your children from who they are as individuals. Be careful not to impose expectations on them based on your needs, interests, or goals.

4. *Begin the process of collaboration.* One of the essential principles of this book is collaboration between you and your children. Once you learn to accept your children for who they are, gain a clearer picture of their unique temperament and style, and begin to make changes in your behavior, it is easier to engage with them in problem-solving discussions of appropriate goals and expectations. When we convey expectations in an accepting, loving, and supportive manner, our children feel motivated to exceed those expectations.

Nurturing Islands of Competence

I (Robert Brooks) coined the term *islands of competence* to describe activities that children engage in successfully and from which they experience enhanced self-confidence and self-esteem. In our books *Raising Resilient Children* and *Nurturing Resilience in Our Children: Answers to the Most Important Parenting Questions*, we point out that recognizing and celebrating our children's skills and competence nurtures a strong, resilient mindset. By assisting your child to develop an island of competence regardless of the skill or ability involved, you strengthen your child's confidence to face challenges, including those posed by engaging in interactions with others. We must refrain from defining success for our children but rather encourage them to define their own accomplishments. We must avoid setting the bar too high for them, lest we place them in situations that lead to failure and low self-esteem. We suggest the following five strategies to help your children experience success and to nurture their islands of competence:

1. *Openly enjoy and celebrate your children's accomplishments.* As our children grow they encounter countless challenges. Although these may seem like small steps to parents, to children they represent major hurdles and advances. Each mastery brings with it a sense of success and achievement, strengthening your child's resolve to deal with new challenges. Children will feel more successful and supported when their achievements are acknowledged and appreciated. For example, acknowledging your shy child's success playing with another child will encourage your child to continue interacting with peers.

2. *Emphasize your children's input in creating success.* Children capable of accepting ownership for their success will develop high self-esteem. A guiding principle must be to provide experiences and offer comments that convey to your children that they are active participants in what transpires in their lives. This is particularly important in shaping your children's mindset and perception of their ability to manage feelings, including anger. As we do so, we perform a balancing act, namely, being available to assist our children but not doing everything for them.

3. *Identify and reinforce your children's islands of competence.* It is important for you to identify and reinforce these islands and appreciate that they may differ from one child to the next.

If we want children to overcome a defeatist mindset we must help them develop self-worth and confidence through successful experiences. Remember also that children will feel greater ownership for their success when they experience these as meaningful to their lives.

4. *Give strengths time to develop.* Many children require time to develop and mature. If your child demonstrates an interest in a particular activity, even if his skills are below average compared to others, it's best to support and nurture the development of these skills within reason. We can never be certain which skills will someday become a child's islands of competence, reinforcing a sense of success and a resilient mindset.

5. *Accept the unique strengths and successes of each child.* Children are aware of our disappointments when they don't meet our expectations and are particularly sensitive when their successes are not viewed as important or relevant by parents. We must, through our words and actions, communicate to our children that we accept them and believe in their capabilities. It is impossible to conceive of children developing a resilient mindset or, for that matter, managing relationships constructively if they do not experience the joy and excitement of success in areas that they and significant others in their lives deem to be important.

Teaching Children to Learn from Mistakes

The ways in which a child understands and responds to mistakes is an integral feature of a resilient mindset. Some children, when faced with mistakes, are motivated to succeed. Others appear defeated. Some children develop a negative view of mistakes, resorting to counterproductive coping strategies such as avoidance, denial, or anger, which interfere with the development of satisfying relationships. There are children who are vulnerable to develop this negative pattern from birth because of their temperament. That is, they appear to come into the world more likely to interpret mistakes as a sign of inadequacy. However, this kind of biological predisposition is reinforced by the negative comments of parents, excessive expectations, and repeated failure.

Following are four strategies that you can use to help your children become increasingly comfortable with the role mistakes play in life. By helping children view mistakes as temporary setbacks and opportunities for learning rather than as indictments of their abilities, you can assist them in developing a resilient mindset.

1. *Serve as a model for dealing with mistakes and setbacks.* Parents are the primary models for children. Our words and actions in response to life's daily challenges affect our children. If children witness parents backing away from challenges and quitting at tasks, they shouldn't be surprised when their children follow the same course of action. Children may not always do what we say, but they often do what we do.

2. *Set realistic expectations.* In our well-intentioned efforts to help our children, we sometimes set the bar too high. By expecting more from children than they are capable of giving, we rob them of the opportunity to learn to view mistakes as challenges. Instead, we create a climate in which children retreat from mistakes, frequently feeling frustrated and angry.

3. *In different ways, emphasize that mistakes are not only accepted but expected.* We must communicate that mistakes are a natural part of life. It is important to develop a positive, less defeatist attitude toward mistakes. If you or your child spill something or forget something, for example, remain calm and verbalize what you or your child might do to lessen the probability of making the same mistake again. And whenever possible, use humor.

4. *Don't make your love contingent on whether your children make mistakes.* Many children believe they are accepted and loved only when they do not make mistakes and fail. Often this belief is intensified when parents hold unrealistic expectations for their children. Unconditional love remains an underlying principle for helping our children learn to deal with mistakes and perceived failure. It is when our children make mistakes and experience setbacks that our ability to be empathic is truly tested. Chil-

dren can deal more effectively with frustration and anger if they are not burdened by the fear of mistakes and failures.

Developing Responsibility, Compassion, and a Social Conscience

Young children are strongly motivated to be helpful. Yet many parents tell us that their children have lost this drive by their middle childhood years. They appear to resist many opportunities to be of assistance unless there is something in it for them. In order for a pattern of helpful behavior to emerge and be maintained, parents must nurture this quality, shaping what may well be an inborn trait into a sense of responsibility, compassion, and social conscience. We must recognize that when children are afforded opportunities to help others, it also provides parents with an opportunity to enhance their child's social skills and interpersonal relationships. Here are four strategies to assist you in this important task.

1. *Serve as a model of responsibility.* As we have discussed before, when we act responsibly and meet our commitments it increases the likelihood our children will behave in a similar way.

2. *Provide opportunities for children to feel they are helping others.* Develop traditions to become a charitable family. A charitable family develops a tradition of involving the entire family in helping others. In doing so you are reinforcing in your children the belief that they are important, they are capable of helping others, they are appreciated, and they can make a difference in their world.

3. *Distribute responsibilities evenly among family members.* It is important for everyone in the family to understand that they each must make a contribution to the daily life of the family.

4. *Take a helicopter view of your child's life.* A helicopter view helps to offset the narrow view we assume sometimes in which we place too much emphasis on one particular area and ignore others. Thus, we may believe that our children are not responsible if they fail to meet a particular task, but in the process we neglect to take into account the many ways they are helping. A helicopter view will challenge you to observe your child's life from a broader perspective. It may also allow you to gain a more realistic picture of your child's many strengths and the ways in which your child is truly contributing to the household and to others.

Summary

A resilient mindset is essential for all children, but even more so for children who face greater challenges and adversity in their lives, such as those struggling to develop an effective social mindset and social skills. Resilience conveys a sense of optimism, ownership, and personal control. It lessens anger and provides children with hope that they will be accepted and liked by others. Parents can serve as charismatic adults in the lives of their children by believing in them and providing them with opportunities that reinforce their islands of competence and feelings of self-worth.

Conclusion

Let's return to Maple Street. At 101 Maple Street, John and his parents have joined a support group for children with Asperger's syndrome. He has met several other kids at the support group functions but continues to seem less interested in developing new friendships compared to his siblings. John's parents continue to encourage him to invite his familiar neighborhood friends over to play, and he has been agreeable and cooperative when friends have come to his house. With these opportunities for social interaction, John and his parents have targeted ways to improve John's eye contact, especially when talking to his friends or when his friends are talking. Another targeted skill identified by John and his parents was to try to be more flexible when his friends want to play with toys or games other than John's submarines. He and his parents practiced ways to respond when a friend suggested

another activity. John would agree to try the friend's suggested activity for a specific period of time, and then discuss with his parents (and when possible and appropriate, with his friend) his thoughts and feelings about how he did or did not like the new activity. With time, John learned to cooperate with his friends and often discovered that he liked new activities his friends had suggested.

At 123 Maple Street, Jimmy and his parents have been working on strategies to help Jimmy feel more comfortable with interacting with his peers. Through the process of environmental engineering described in Step 3, Jimmy has had several new friends over to play. When discussing his thoughts and feelings with his parents, he has learned to recognize that he often seems to worry about not knowing what to say or do when playing with his peers. Jimmy and his parents identified his strengths and turned those strengths into positive thoughts and feelings, which in turn gave him more confidence when targeting skills for actions or reactions in social settings. One of Jimmy's strengths was a tremendous knowledge of baseball and some athletic skill (he was described by his coach as "one of the best on his team"). With this strength in mind, Jimmy practiced with his parents approaching others to start a conversation by asking what they liked to do or what sports they liked to play. They also practiced saying "I don't know" if someone approached him and asked him about something he didn't know about or didn't know how to answer. With these two practice skills, Jimmy felt a little more at ease when having new friends over to play, and as he practiced these skills in other social settings as well, his confidence in talking to others improved tremendously.

At 127 Maple Street, Melanie and her family have been working on finding ways to make and keep friends. Melanie gave her parents the OK to talk to her teacher, and when doing so her parents discovered that Melanie attempted to socialize with her peers at all the wrong moments. Melanie's teacher reported that Melanie seemed like a sweet and sincere child, but had difficulty recognizing when peers were giving her hints to back off. Melanie tended to barge into others' conversations and often had to be reminded not to talk to her classmates during work time. Although she had no problems initiating conversation, she sometimes seemed to talk "at" her peers and tended to talk mostly about herself.

Melanie and her parents made initial goals to help Melanie identify "good" versus "not so good" times to start talking to others. One of Melanie's strengths was feeling comfortable approaching and starting a conversation with oth-

ers. However, one of her targeted skills was to think more about the timing, which included both thinking about the setting and practicing interpersonal timing. Another targeted skill was to try to ask questions to learn about her friends, such as their likes or dislikes or what they've been doing, rather than just telling her friends facts or information about herself.

Down the block at 147 Maple Street, Shannon's parents had some initial difficulty getting Shannon to identify actions and reactions in her behavior that tended to intimidate or alienate her neighbors and classmates. With careful, empathic, and nonjudgmental problem solving, Shannon eventually confided to her parents that she felt that none of her peers would like her anyway, so she didn't feel it would do any good to be nice to them. With this information brought to light, Shannon's parents sought the help of the school counselor, who referred them to a psychologist. While working with the psychologist, it was discovered that Shannon had longstanding negative self-thoughts, especially about her own skills and abilities.

Shannon and her parents, with the assistance of the psychologist, worked on addressing issues of self-esteem, resilience, and confidence. Outside of the therapy setting, Shannon and her parents discussed and practiced more positive ways to interact with peers. Shannon agreed to try an art class because she had been interested in art for a long time but had always feared she "wouldn't be any good at it." Shannon met another girl in the class about the same age, and they arranged to meet for breakfast every Saturday morning before the art class. Shannon developed a greater sense of things she could do and feel competent, and with the exposure to settings where she could meet others with similar interests, she made a connection with another child.

———

We hope that this book has helped you and your child recognize the wonderful traits and skills you possess as individuals and as a family. We also hope the book is a valuable guide as you begin the journey to making positive changes in your child's social skills, abilities, and interactions. We sincerely wish that this book makes the often complex, sometimes difficult navigation of the social and interpersonal realm less daunting for those who wish to further explore and experience it with more confidence, hope, and resilience. As always, we appreciate feedback and ideas for improving this book, and we wish you and your family the very best.

Appendix A

Understanding and Developing
Social Skills in Children

A Guide for Medical and Mental Health Professionals

More often than not, children presenting to mental health professionals experience problems with social interaction. For some, the problems result from low-incidence, high-impact behaviors. Some conditions, such as attention deficit hyperactivity disorder or oppositional defiance and conduct disorder, often lead to impulsive and aggressive patterns of behavior that disturb others, leading to social rejection. Conditions such as depression, anxiety, learning disabilities, or various forms of pervasive developmental disorder often result in high-incidence, low-impact behaviors. Children with these conditions often struggle to exhibit appropriate social skills. Children with the latter set of conditions may know what to do but not consistently do it. Improving social skills and social relations is a frequent goal in counseling and other therapeutic endeavors for children presenting to mental health professionals.

This brief appendix provides an overview of social skills and discussions of assessment, treatment models, and ways of developing effective social skills. The Resources section at the end of the appendix includes several research demonstrated social skills programs geared toward mental health professionals.

Overview of Social Skills

Social skills are discrete, learned behaviors exhibited by an individual for the purpose of performing a specific task (Sheridan, 1998). These behaviors are observable, measurable, and concrete. In contrast, *social competence* is concerned primarily with the evaluative judgments of others (Gresham, 1986) and is typically conceptualized in terms of the opinions of others as receivers of social overtures.

Sheridan and Walker (1999) present a framework of what they term *social skillfulness,* representing a combination of social skills and social competence. In this model, social skills are "goal directed learned behaviors allowing an individual to interact and function effectively in a variety of social contexts" (page 233). To be socially skillful, a child must first learn important social behaviors necessary in a variety of situations and then learn to relate in a way that is acceptable to others in a variety of social situations.

Of all the tasks a child must master, establishing and maintaining meaningful relationships with peers and adults is perhaps the most important. Successful peer relationships help children feel worthy, competent, and connected, filling many important needs and forming a cornerstone of a resilient mindset. Peer relations also set the stage for taking others' perspective and building mutual understanding. To develop friendships, children must accomplish at least two related tasks: learn to relate in a way that is acceptable to peers and learn the skills of friendship necessary for relationships in later life.

Socially competent children exhibit a number of key characteristics. Such children can initiate interactions successfully. They know how to join groups. They use a variety of interpersonal tactics rather than relying on a single similar behavior in every social setting. They demonstrate a balance in their social communicative interactions. They engage in alternative turn-taking exchanges with an understanding of timing and roles within interactions. They know how to maintain a conversation, listen, and attend to others. Well-liked children are also able to share, offer assistance, and give praise and compliments, many of the qualities that define a resilient mindset. Children with a competent so-

cialization mindset have a history of engaging in productive social activities and, most important, are effective problem solvers in social interaction. They recognize a variety of behavioral alternatives and can select the strategy or behavior at any given time that holds the greatest potential for successful problem resolution.

Socially unskilled children, in contrast, lack one or more (sometimes many) of these competencies. Additionally, some may be socially withdrawn or socially aggressive. Both groups exhibit an inability to act effectively and appropriately within their social environment. Socially withdrawn children are often neglected and isolated from their peer group. Socially aggressive children are often rejected and behave in aversive ways that lead peers to distance themselves.

Socially withdrawn children tend to be isolated, shy, and passive. Often they are comfortable being alone. However, some recognize their isolation and are bothered by it, which can lead to feelings of inadequacy, incompetence, and helplessness. An acute onset of social withdrawal may represent one of the most visible markers of the beginnings of a major depressive disorder. Children demonstrating social withdrawal on a chronic basis often possess few strategies available for solving social problems. They frequently develop a helpless approach as their efforts engaging peers eventually build a long history of failure and frustration. They struggle to elicit positive responses from peers and eventually, in a self-fulfilling manner, become increasingly passive, anticipating that future attempts will meet with continued failure.

Socially aggressive children, on the other hand, can be verbally and physically assaultive. They may bully, tease, provoke, or quarrel. They tend to ignore and violate the rights of others, which in mental health settings often leads to diagnoses of oppositional defiance and/or conduct disorder. Often these children have appropriate social skills but use them in an inappropriate way. Their tactics may be effective but the children frequently act inappropriately and are disliked by others. For some children, this pattern of behavior results from responding impulsively. For other children, socially provocative behavior is often planned. These children exhibit few prosocial behaviors such as helping, sharing, or cooperating, and are at risk to develop antisocial patterns. They use aggression and threat to gain control of others. These children often attribute their misfortunes to the hostile behaviors of others, misinterpret social cues, and then respond in a provocative, aggressive way, creating a self-fulfilling prophecy and outcome.

Giler (2002) notes that children with developmental problems, such as learning disability, ADHD, and likely pervasive developmental disorder, do not read facial expressions or body language well, may misinterpret the use and meaning of pitch, and may misunderstand the use of personal space. Their ability to initiate conversations, ask questions, show interest in others and extend invitations, give compliments, smile, and laugh are often impaired due to their dependence on specific developmental weaknesses, many of which relate to language.

Evaluating Social Skill Problems

It is beyond the scope of this appendix to provide an in-depth overview of social skill assessment; the Resources section offers several models. Elliott and Busse (1991) provide a framework for social skills consultation and evaluation using the acronym DATE (*define, assess,*

treat, and *evaluate*). In this model, social behaviors are targeted in social skills interventions through identification and definition in observable, specific terms. They are assessed using a multimethod, multisource, multisetting approach. Treatment strategies are developed based on the child's needs and demonstration of skill or performance deficits. Progress with the intervention is evaluated empirically with similar assessment strategies used to identify social skills problems.

Assessment begins with a general and global evaluation and then is narrowed to specify and clarify targets for intervention. Social skills are often evaluated in mental health settings as part of a broad assessment of a child's behavior, cognitive ability, and current functioning. Professionals interested in a statistically derived assessment tool should consider Gresham and Elliott's social skills rating system (1990) and the Walker-McConnell Scale of Social Competence (1988).

Rating scale assessment is helpful in obtaining data regarding important components of a child's social skills from a variety of sources. Such scales can provide estimates of the frequency of behaviors, indicate skill and performance deficits, and assist in creating guidelines for intervention. Input from the child and direct observation can also be helpful in providing an overview of a child's social functioning. A rating model developed by Gresham and Elliott (1990), the Social Skills Rating System, allows professionals to identify four types of problems:

1. Children lack social skills.

2. Children have social skills but don't use them.

3. Children lack social skills and exhibit other interfering problems (such as language disorder or anxiety).

4. Children have appropriate social skills but interfering problem behaviors prevent the efficient use of these skills. This group often has what is referred to as *self-control social skill deficits*. They know what to do but do not stop and think for sufficient duration to do what they know in the right situation.

The following informal questionnaire describes a set of basic social skills and behaviors. In lieu of using a standardized social skills assessment tool (such as the aforementioned Social Skills Rating System, for example), you can use this tool with parents during the course of a history session to screen basic social skills and behavior. Identified weaknesses can be targeted for intervention when a treatment plan is created.

Social Skills Assessment

Read the description of each item and check off the answer that best describes your opinion of the child's abilities.

Part I

The child . . .

❑ Yes ❑ No   appears socially isolated, spending a large proportion of time engaged in solitary activities.

❑ Yes ❑ No   interacts less with others, appearing shy, timid, or overanxious.

❑ Yes ❑ No   complains of having no one to play with.

❑ Yes ❑ No   spends less time involved with other children due to an apparent lack of social skills.

❑ Yes ❑ No   has fewer friends than others dueto negative, bossy, or annoying behaviors.

❑ Yes ❑ No   has fewer friends than others due to awkward or bizarre behaviors.

❑ Yes ❑ No   disturbs others by teasing, provoking, fighting, or interruptions.

❑ Yes ❑ No   is argumentative and needs to have the last words in verbal exchanges.

❑ Yes ❑ No   is aggressive toward others.

❑ Yes ❑ No   manipulates or threatens.

Part II

For each item, indicate the level of skill the child exhibits, using the scale below.

1 Very poor at this skill
2 Demonstrates this skill as well as others
3 Exhibits this skill better than others

The child . . .

_____ demonstrates empathy.

_____ demonstrates the capacity for humor.

_____ expresses frustration and anger effectively.

_____ gains access to ongoing activities with peers.

_____ asserts rights and needs appropriately.

_____ expresses wishes and preferences clearly.

_____ approaches others positively.

_____ shares.

_____ plays games successfully with others.

_____ works cooperatively with peers.

_____ offers help to others.

_____ begins a conversation appropriately.

_____ listens during conversation.

_____ ends a conversation appropriately.

_____ asks questions appropriately.

_____ says "please" and "thank you."

_____ apologizes when a mistake is made

_____ accepts a compliment.

_____ gives a compliment.

_____ interprets body language.

_____ seeks help from others appropriately.

_____ joins an ongoing activity with others.

_____ takes turns appropriately.

_____ compromises with others appropriately.

_____ maintains eye contact when interacting with others.

_____ recognizes appropriate personal space when approaching others.

Developing Social Skills

This book lends itself easily to adaptation and use in a mental health setting. Professionals can use a variety of strategies in group or individual counseling to develop appropriate social skills, including modeling; coaching through direct verbal instruction and discussion; social problem solving involving a combination of cognitive, emotional, and behavioral factors; and operant techniques involving manipulation of social antecedents (altering the social environment) and consequences (providing appropriate reinforcement contingent on demonstration of desired behavior).

Social skills interventions are effective only if they generalize to naturally occurring, meaningful social situations. Mental health professionals must make an effort to provide opportunities for generalization, otherwise it is not likely that skills taught in a controlled office setting will find their way into everyday use. As Sheridan (1995) notes, generalization can be facilitated by making the training situation as comparable to the natural environment as possible; facing consequences that approximate those that occur in the natural environment; reinforcing the use of positive social skills in new and appropriate social situations; reinforcing social goal setting, accurate self-report, and self-monitoring of performance; and finally, including peers during training.

References

Elliott, S.N., & Busse, R.T. (1991). Social skills assessment and intervention with children and adolescents. *School Psychology International*, 12, 63-83.

Giler, J.Z. (2002). *Socially ADDept: A Manual for Parents of Children with ADHD and/or Learning Disabilitie*s. Santa Barbara, CA: CES Publications.

Gresham, F.M. (1986). Conceptual issues in the assessment of social competence in children. In P. Strain, M. Guralnick, & H.M. Walker (Eds.). *Children's social behavior: Development, assessment and modification.* New York: Academic Press.

Gresham, F.M., & Elliott, S.N. (1990). *Social skills rating system.* Circle Pines, MN: American Guidance Services.

Sheridan, S.M. (1995). *The tough kid social skills book.* Longmont, CO: Sopris West.

Sheridan, S.M. (1998). *Why don't they like me? Helping your child make and keep friends.* Longmont, CO: Sopris West.

Sheridan, S.M., & Walker, D. (1999). Social skills in context: Considerations for assessment, intervention, and generalization. In C.R. Reynolds & T.B. Gutkin (Eds.). *The handbook of school psychology (3ʳᵈ ed.).* New York: Wiley.

Walker, H.M., Todis, B., Holmes, D., & Horton, G. (1988). *The Walker social skills curriculum: The ACCESS program.* Austin, TX: Pro-Ed.

Resources

Giler, J.Z. (2002). *Socially ADDept: A Manual for Parents of Children with ADHD and/or Learning Disabilities.* Santa Barbara, CA: CES Publications.

Goldstein, A.P., & McGinnis, E. (1997). *Skillstreaming the adolescent: New strategies and perspectives for teaching prosocial skills.* Champaign, IL: Research Press.

Gresham, F.M., & Elliott, S.N. (1990). *Social skills rating system.* Circle Pines, MN: American Guidance Services.

Hazel, J.S., Bragg-Schumaker, J., Sherman, J.A., & Sheldon-Wildgen, J. (1981). *ASSET: A social skills program for adolescents.* (Video.) Champaign, IL: Research Press.

Jackson, N.F., Jackson, D.A., & Monroe, C. (1993). *Getting along with others: Teaching social effectiveness to children.* Champaign, IL: Research Press.

Lavoie, R. (2005). *It's so much work to be your friend: Helping the child with learning disabilities find social success.* New York: Simon & Schuster.

McGinnis, E., & Goldstein, A.P. (1997). *Skillstreaming the elementary school child: New strategies and perspectives for teaching prosocial skills.* Champaign, IL: Research Press.

McGinnis, E., & Goldstein, A.P. (2003). *Skillstreaming in early childhood: New strategies and perspectives for teaching prosocial skills.* Champaign, IL: Research Press.

Sheridan, S.M. (1995). *The tough kids social skills book.* Longmont, CO: Sopris West.

Sheridan, S.M. (1998). *Why don't they like me? Helping your child make and keep friends.* Longmont, CO: Sopris West.

Siperstein, G.N., & Rickards, E.P. (2004). *Promoting social success: A curriculum for children with special needs.* Baltimore: Paul H. Brookes Publishing Co.

Walker, H.M., McConnell, S., Holmes, D., Todis, B., Walker, J., & Golden, N. (1993). *The Walker social skills curriculum: The ACCEPTS program.* Austin, TX: Pro-Ed.

Appendix B

Understanding and Developing
Social Skills in Children:
A Guide for Educators

Socialization difficulties represent one of the most challenging problems facing teachers in kindergarten through high school classrooms. Youth experiencing difficulty with socialization in the school environment often have language, learning, emotional, or behavioral problems as well. Thus, social skills problems rarely occur in isolation, making them complicated to understand, evaluate, and improve.

Improving social skills and social relations is a frequent goal in the classroom. This brief appendix is designed to assist educators with this goal by providing an overview of social skills and a discussion of models to develop effective social skills. In addition, the Resources section at the end of this appendix includes several citations of research-demonstrated social skills programs available for educators.

Socially skilled children possess effective social skills and competence. To be socially skill-ful a child must first learn a range of important social behaviors, exhibit them in a variety of acceptable situations. These skills must be generalized from one setting to the next. Children must understand social situations and know what is an appropriate response in a particular situation. Socialization difficulties represent one of the most challenging problems facing teachers in kindergarten through high school classrooms. Youth experiencing difficulty with socialization in the classroom and related school environment often struggle with language, learning, emotional, or behavioral problems as well. Thus, social skills problems rarely occur in isolation, making them complicated to understand, evaluate, and improve. For example, for some children social problems result from low-incidence, high-impact behaviors. They are impulsive or aggressive. Their behavior disturbs others, leading to social rejection. Other children exhibit high-incidence, low-impact behaviors. They struggle to exhibit appropriate social skills but are not necessarily rejected by their peers. Children with the first set of skills often know what to do but don't consistently do it in social situations. Children with the second set of problems are often skill deficient. Improving social skills and social relations is frequently goal in the classroom. This brief handout will provide an overview of social skills and a discussion of models to develop effective social skills. There are a number of research-demonstrated social skills programs available for educators. These are cited in the Resources section at the end of this handout.

Background Overview of Social Skills

Social skills are discrete, learned behaviors exhibited by an individual for the purpose of performing a specific task (Sheridan, 1998). These behaviors are observable, measurable, and concrete. In contrast, *social competence* is concerned primarily with the evaluative judgments of others (Gresham, 1986) and is typically conceptualized in terms of the opinions of others as receivers of social overtures.

To be socially skillful a child must learn a range of important social behaviors, then exhibit them in a variety of acceptable situations. These skills must be generalized from one setting to the next.

Of all the tasks a child must master, establishing and maintaining meaningful relationships with peers and adults is perhaps the most important. Successful peer relationships help children feel worthy, competent, and connected, filling many important needs and forming a cornerstone of a resilient mindset. Peer relations also set the

stage for taking others' perspective and building mutual understanding.

To develop friendships children must relate in ways that are acceptable and master the skills necessary to be socially attractive to others. Unfortunately, some children are *neglected* (liked by few, disliked by few) and others are *rejected* (liked by few, disliked by many). Neglected children can at times be victimized by bullies, but most children simply don't seek out neglected children. They don't mind partnering with them on projects, but wouldn't choose them as partners. Rejected children often exhibit aggressive behaviors that lead other children to give them a wide berth. *Controversial children* (liked by many, disliked by many) typically possess certain talents such as athletics that make them sought out despite the fact that they behave in ways that disturb and disrupt others. Within the classroom, children who are *popular* are liked by many and disliked by few. They often possess an easygoing style, are empathic, communicate well, and are willing to help others.

Popular children can initiate interactions successfully. They know how to join groups. They use a variety of interpersonal tactics rather than relying on a single similar behavior each time. They also demonstrate a balance in their social communicative interactions. They engage in alternative turn taking with an understanding of timing and roles. They know how to maintain a conversation, listen, and attend to others. Well-liked children are also able to share, offer assistance, and give praise and compliments, many of the qualities that define a resilient mindset. Children with a competent socialization mindset have a history of engaging in productive social activities and, most important, are effective problem solvers in social interaction. They recognize a variety of behavioral alternatives and can select the strategy or behavior at any given time that holds the greatest potential for successful problem resolution.

Socially unskilled children, in contrast, lack one or more (sometimes many) of these competencies. Additionally, some may be socially withdrawn or socially aggressive. Both groups exhibit an inability to act effectively and appropriately within their social environment. Socially withdrawn children are often neglected and isolated from their peer group. Socially aggressive children are often rejected and behave in aversive ways that lead peers to distance themselves.

Socially withdrawn children tend to be isolated, shy, and passive. Often they are comfortable being alone. However, some recognize their isolation and are bothered by it, which can lead to feelings of inadequacy, incompetence, and helplessness. An acute onset of social withdrawal may represent one of the most visible markers of the beginnings of a major depressive disorder. Children demonstrating social withdrawal on a chronic basis often possess few strategies available for solving social problems. They frequently develop a helpless approach as their efforts engaging peers eventually build a long history of failure and frustration. They struggle to elicit positive responses from peers and eventually, in a self-fulfilling manner, become increasingly passive, anticipating that future attempts will meet with continued failure.

Socially aggressive children, on the other hand, can be verbally and physically assaultive. They may bully, tease, provoke, or quarrel. They tend to ignore and violate the rights of others, which leads to patterns of oppositional and delinquent behavior. Often these children possess appropriate social skills but use them in inap-

propriate ways. Their tactics may be effective but the children are frequently inappropriate and disliked by others. For some children, this pattern results from impulsive responding. For other children, socially provocative behavior is often planned. These children exhibit few prosocial behaviors such as helping, sharing, or cooperating, and are at risk to develop antisocial patterns. They use aggression and threat to gain control of others. These children often attribute their misfortunes to the hostile behaviors of others, misinterpret social cues, and then respond in a provocative, aggressive way, creating a self-fulfilling prophecy and outcome.

Approximately 20 percent of students in every elementary through high school classroom will experience some type of developmental problem, such as a learning disability, attention deficit hyperactivity disorder, or pervasive developmental disorder. These conditions may impede their ability to develop effective social skills. This group of children—as well as those experiencing emotional problems, including depression and anxiety—often do not read facial expressions or body language accurately or appropriately. They may misinterpret the use and meaning of vocal pitch or misunderstand the use of personal space. Their ability to initiate conversation, ask questions, show interest in others, give compliments, smile, and laugh may be impaired due to their dependence on developmentally weak skills, many of which are related to language.

Evaluating Social Skills Problems

Teachers must be good generalists. Like pediatricians or family practitioners, they must know something about everything, yet cannot possibly know everything about anything. Classroom teachers can and do quickly recognize socially incompetent children. This process of identification within the natural setting is an appropriate first step for identifying children in need of assistance. It is beyond the charge of educators and the scope of this appendix to provide an in-depth overview of social skills assessment. Classroom consultants often use a model in which social skill problems are targeted through identification and definition in observable, specific terms. These behaviors are then evaluated using a multimethod, multisource, multisetting approach beyond just the classroom. Treatment strategies are developed based on the child's needs and demonstration of skill or performance deficits. Progress with the intervention is evaluated empirically with similar assessment strategies used to identify social skills problems.

If you suspect that a child or adolescent in your classroom is struggling with socialization, the first step is to communicate with parents and a school-based consultant such as the school counselor, school psychologist, or special educator. These individuals will want specifics from you. Thus, before you make a referral it is important to go through a process by which specific social skill weaknesses can be identified and defined beyond just the general observation of "social problems." The following screening questionnaire will help you gather narrative information concerning a child's social skills and abilities.

Social Skills Screening Questionnaire

Read the description of each item and check off the answer that best describes your opinion of the child's abilities.

Part I

The child . . .

❑ Yes ❑ No   appears socially isolated, spending a large proportion of time engaged in solitary activities.

❑ Yes ❑ No   interacts less with others, appearing shy, timid, or overanxious.

❑ Yes ❑ No   complains of having no one to play with.

❑ Yes ❑ No   spends less time involved with other children due to an apparent lack of social skills.

❑ Yes ❑ No   has fewer friends than others due to negative, bossy, or annoying behaviors.

❑ Yes ❑ No   has fewer friends than others due to awkward or bizarre behaviors.

❑ Yes ❑ No   disturbs others by teasing, provoking, fighting, or interruptions.

❑ Yes ❑ No   is argumentative and needs to have the last words in verbal exchanges.

❑ Yes ❑ No   is aggressive toward others.

❑ Yes ❑ No   manipulates or threatens.

Part II

For each item, indicate the level of skill the child exhibits, using the scale below.

1 Very poor at this skill
2 Demonstrates this skill as well as others
3 Exhibits this skill better than others

The child . . .

_____ demonstrates empathy.

_____ demonstrates the capacity for humor.

_____ expresses frustration and anger effectively.

_____ gains access to ongoing activities with peers.

_____ asserts rights and needs appropriately.

_____ expresses wishes and preferences clearly.

_____ approaches others positively.

_____ shares.

_____ plays games successfully with others.

_____ works cooperatively with peers.

_____ offers help to others.

_____ begins a conversation appropriately.

_____ listens during conversation.

_____ ends a conversation appropriately.

_____ asks questions appropriately.

_____ says "please" and "thank you."

_____ apologizes when a mistake is made

_____ accepts a compliment.

_____ gives a compliment.

_____ interprets body language.

_____ seeks help from others appropriately.

_____ joins an ongoing activity with others.

_____ takes turns appropriately.

_____ compromises with others appropriately.

_____ maintains eye contact when interacting with others.

_____ recognizes appropriate personal space when approaching others.

With this questionnaire completed, you are in a much better position to explain in functional ways the concerns you have about a child's social skills and competence. Though this questionnaire reflects your subjective opinions and is not scored, it gathers important information about a variety of components of social skills. This rating scale provides an estimate of the frequency of behaviors and begins to identify goals for intervention.

As you think about a particular child's social problems, consider the model developed by Gresham and Elliott (1990). The Social Skills Rating System allows professionals to identify four types of problems:

1. Children lack social skills.

2. Children have social skills but don't use them.

3. Children lack social skills and exhibit other interfering problems (such as language disorder or anxiety).

4. Children have appropriate social skills but interfering problem behaviors prevent the efficient use of these skills. This group often has what is referred to as *self-control social skill deficits*. They know what to do but do not stop and think for sufficient duration to do what they know in the right situation.

Developing Social Skills

Although this book is directed at parents, classroom educators can easily modify and use the strategies in school with groups or with an individual child. Strategies including modeling; coaching through direct verbal instruction and discussion; social problem solving involving a combination of cognitive, emotional, and behavioral factors; and operant techniques involving manipulation of social antecedents (altering the social environment) and consequences (providing appropriate reinforcement contingent on demonstration of desired behavior) can be attempted.

It is important to remember that social skills interventions are effective only if they generalize to naturally occurring, meaningful social situations. The classroom is often a good place to provide opportunity for generalization. If one of your students is participating in an individual or group social skills development program, be prepared to provide opportunities in the classroom for the child to demonstrate and generalize the skills being taught. The Resources section that follows contains a number of excellent resources that can be applied to the classroom.

Resources

Giler, J.Z. (2002). *Socially ADDept: A Manual for Parents of Children with ADHD and/or Learning Disabilities.* Santa Barbara, CA: CES Publications.

Goldstein, A.P., & McGinnis, E. (1997). *Skillstreaming the adolescent: New strategies and perspectives for teaching prosocial skills.* Champaign, IL: Research Press.

Gresham, F.M. (1986). Conceptual issues in the assessment of social competence in children. In P. Strain, M. Guralnick, & H.M. Walker (Eds.). *Children's social behavior: Development, assessment and modification.* New York: Academic Press.

Gresham, F.M., & Elliott, S.N. (1990). *Social skills rating system.* Circle Pines, MN: American Guidance Services.

Hazel, J.S., Bragg-Schumaker, J., Sherman, J.A., & Sheldon-Wildgen, J. (1981). *ASSET: A social skills program for adolescents.* (Video.) Champaign, IL: Research Press.

Jackson, N.F., Jackson, D.A., & Monroe, C. (1993). *Getting along with others: Teaching social effectiveness to children.* Champaign, IL: Research Press.

Lavoie, R. (2005). *It's so much work to be your friend: Helping the child with learning disabilities find social success.* New York: Simon & Schuster.

McGinnis, E., & Goldstein, A.P. (1997). *Skillstreaming the elementary school child: New strategies and perspectives for teaching prosocial skills.* Champaign, IL: Research Press.

McGinnis, E., & Goldstein, A.P. (2003). *Skillstreaming in early childhood: New strategies and perspectives for teaching prosocial skills.* Champaign, IL: Research Press.

Sheridan, S.M. (1995). *The tough kids social skills book.* Longmont, CO: Sopris West.

Sheridan, S.M. (1998). *Why don't they like me? Helping your child make and keep friends.* Longmont, CO: Sopris West.

Siperstein, G.N., & Rickards, E.P. (2004). *Promoting social success: A curriculum for children with special needs.* Baltimore: Paul H. Brookes Publishing Co.

Walker, H.M., McConnell, S., Holmes, D., Todis, B., Walker, J., & Golden, N. (1993). *The Walker social skills curriculum: The ACCEPTS program.* Austin, TX: Pro-Ed.

Walker, H.M., Todis, B., Holmes, D., & Horton, G. (1988). *The Walker social skills curriculum: The ACCESS program.* Austin, TX: Pro-Ed.

Index